ALL AT SEA

Another Side of Paradise

JULIAN SAYARER

A

For the fish

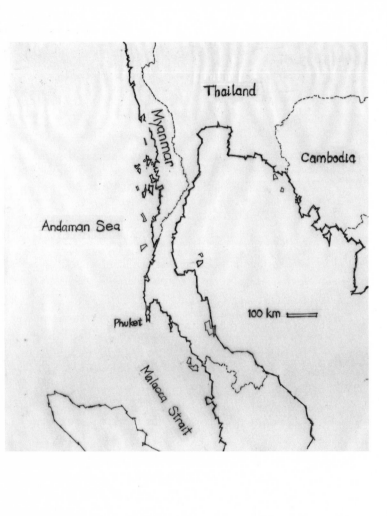

Prologue

The beaches were strewn with bodies. Washed up naked, dressed in rags … intoxicated, drugged, punch-drunk. Westerners littered the white sands, giddy, high on Shangri-La. The Thai called them *farang*. Tourists. Casualties lay dotted all about, lifeless, their skin scorched by sun. Wrapped around dozens of legs were the weeping wounds of unlucky motorbike passengers, calves and ankles branded by the hot stack of an exhaust pipe touched accidentally in a whiff of burnt flesh. Others had fallen off the back altogether, picked themselves up with maps of road-rash strafed across their skin in serrated mazes. Soles had been accidentally slit open as people boogied barefoot on beaches mined with shards of their own broken glass and plastic bottles. First aiders buckled under the weight of too few medics for too many wounded, and on bamboo stretchers, patients writhed, their feet wrapped in white towels shifting quickly scarlet around bleeding feet. Cries of agony went lifting into the night, bottom lips warbled and concerned friends kept vigil. Iodine was washed yellow into wounds, oxygenated water stung with shrieks. Damn but it looked like the fucking Somme, Juno or Sword … Wilfred Owen, Siegfried Sassoon … all conscripted to Thailand and charged with having enough fun to make the free world feel free again.

In Sanksrit, Kanji, Aramaic and Chinese scripts, philosophies of life were printed with blue-green ink on white skin. Symbols professing heartfelt mantras were tattooed behind earlobes, at the tops of spines, along the twin tendons that ran from wrists into hands in a forlorn quest for originality. What was needed, what was really called for, was a new bit of anatomy coming on to the market: an update, a new limb into the gene pool, for too many identical bodies all had owners after the same thing. Entire boatfuls kept unloading. New fish were sure to arrive with the next dawn, and all would storm tropical beaches in this D-Day for a new age. They waged a war against anomie: rock-solid, dye-cast anomie. Born of a stale world in right angles of glass and steel, there they were, desperately seeking to carve out legend among Thailand's rougher edges. A local entrepreneur stirred a wooden paddle through a trough of drink: hard liquor and carbonated soda. He handed it over, selling it to the farang in sandcastle buckets with straws that, for just a handful of dollars, gave the option for those dispossessed, doomed youths to buy back a moment of childhood.

All along the shoreline petrol-soaked rags stood on the ends of charred sticks, from which flames shone and danced to the electronic beat of loudspeakers. Effluent and vomit flooded from makeshift toilets, running towards the sea, while all around lust beckoned and tongues looked for meaning in the mouths of strangers. Phones and cameras, extended at the end of each grasping reach, captured it all so that everyone photographed everything and looked at nothing. Overhead hung long, dense lines of telephone cables: wrapped like creepers, vines, they went entwined between concrete poles. Tied back towards the motherland, every last message of these new prophets was all set to make it out to a satellite, ensuring that none upon the beach ever felt too far from home. Roaring in from overhead, on the hot strip of the runway, the plane touched down.

PART I

PHUKET

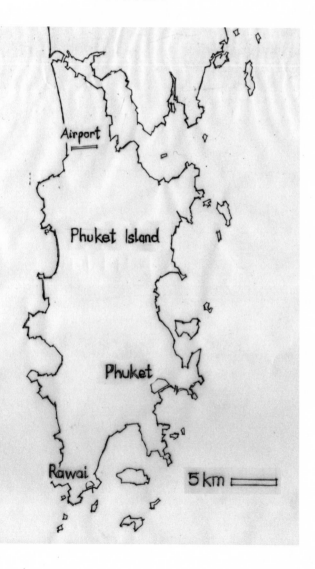

Gitano – Tuesday, dusk

Let's begin with Gitano, go from there. He picked us up at the airport, had even written our names on a small sign where he waited in the arrivals lounge, as if the whole thing were reputable.

'Reinard sends his apologies, but he couldn't be here to meet you. He had to find a translator for the project.'

'We thought he had one already?' Jake replied, concerned.

'So did he.'

And with that, things started as they would go on.

Evening came down equator-quick, white lights blazing on the construction site of a Thai-Italian consortium sinking a tunnel under the Phuket highway. Gitano drove fast, Gitano drove dumb ... one of those guys who tells you he's a good driver with a clenched fist, follows up with *'because I react very quick!'* He got up close, agitated on the accelerator. Tailgating every vehicle, he forced his way through gaps that weren't there, then hit hard at the horn when they closed on him too fast. Dressed in a vest and jeans, he had a sharp face, darting, keen: eyes bright but everything else washed in resignation. Across his arms and chest I looked into the dashboard, where there were small drifts of sand along its dials. The petrol gauge was near flat, right down towards red, but you got the impression Gitano knew how far he could push it. A few of the other dials looked broken, but the kilometres ticked over, turning round so that 199,998 became 199,999 and then the top of that 2 and all those new zeros came up hesitantly like their own quantitative sunrise. I wondered how many of those 200,000 belonged to Gitano, where they'd taken him, who he'd met.

'Where you from?' I asked. Jake was in the back, taking in the world through the window, leaving the talking to me.

'East Germany.' He turned away from me, looked out the window with a solemnity that seemed almost disappointed or defiant about reunification.

'Why d'you leave?'

'It's changed. I was from Berlin, but now Berlin is different. Full of Turks.'

I smiled, ready for a moment of power, ready for the squirm. He deserved it, for that one.

'I'm Turkish. Half-Turkish.'

Gitano looked across. The poor guy, you knew he had no luck left in him, I felt sorry to have done it. He guffawed, swallowed his foot, up to his knee.

'The new generations are different. I have lots of …' He began again. 'The older generations were more respectful. I have lots of Turkish friends, black friends' – Gitano starts coming over all rainbow – 'I have friends from all over the world!'

He raises his arm in the air, right out in front of him in a palm-down recognition of the Führer. You have to pity the Germans … they really have to go above and beyond when it comes to convincing people they're not racists.

Gitano let out a half-hearted salute, as if to make clear what he was not. 'I'm not a Nazi… none of that bullshit.'

When the words *I'm not a Nazi* are exchanged in the first minutes of meeting a guy, that's when you know things are going badly. We changed the subject pretty quick. I let him off light.

'How do you know Reinard? You friends?'

'He's a very good man … a good heart.' And then Gitano got on with what was important, his preferred subject, himself.

'Reinard always knew he could trust me. I was a performer.' He smiled fondly for better times. 'I was a juggler … but not a regular juggler, a high-speed juggler, with lots of balls, going very high.'

We drove on: Jake still looking out the window, me not sure what to say, Gitano looking right at me, forgetting the road.

'But I need to stop drinking so much.' He sighed, waving his hand and letting it fall at his over-round stomach. 'My juggling isn't as good any more. I lost my focus. I need to get back into training, but I'm always driving, and in the evenings people want to go to the bar to get drunk together!'

He looked across, 'I performed all over the world. I performed in Moscow, in Havana.'

'Always juggling?' I asked, checked that I was hearing right.

'Yes! Always juggling!' Gitano grew ever more uninterested in the road, as if it had been a long time since anyone had cared enough to listen. 'I performed with very famous people … *with Rostropovich*!'

Gitano lightened, forgot the present and remembered the good days, back when he was something special and it was all going to work out for him.

'You know Rostropovich?' he leaned in eagerly, 'With me juggling and him on the cello.' He kissed his fingers, scarcely able to believe the memory. 'I was one of the most respected performers in the Soviet Union.'

I smiled, gave a nod, stopped babysitting the man and did as Jake – checked out of the conversation. Nothing was about to make Gitano feel any better about his present compared to his past. The palm trees passed over us. I still remembered Heathrow, the A4: six thousand miles and only a few hours' sleep ago. It was a strange transition, quicker than I was used to. The sky went purple, orange at the horizon, like a bright ribbon wrapping a box full of dusk. And the palm trees passed over us, and over us. Horns fired, motor scooters with bags of rice over the saddle and their taillights trailing out behind, red streams scratched into night.

Gitano reclined in his seat, got on with the driving, one of those washed-up souls who were never at home no matter where you put them. A German stuck in the tropics. 'This country!' – he threw his hands up in the air, hitting the brakes as a slender space between a car and the small van of a farmer shifted from narrow to impassable – 'This country needs to change.'

He didn't realise it himself, but more change was the last thing Gitano needed … he'd already seen too much of the stuff. Gitano's face betrayed how poorly things had gone for him since his juggling days. A face starved of smiles, his hair in a crew cut, all the values he had energy left for were the coloured bracelets and a few charitable rubber bands on his wrists. I suspected that Gitano needed the dysfunction of Thailand to satisfy his need to complain; one of those guys who is already turning, going bitter, by the time he leaves the developed world for the tropics, but times it right, so that everything he then finds there can be blamed on the place he arrived in and neither himself nor the place he left. A few years younger and I'd have been different, would have had more sympathy for a life not working out as it might have done, more interest in sharing his glory years, encouraging him to speak. These days I've less energy for it. Eventually you meet too many lost causes.

The Sage – night

Gitano left us outside a hotel in the town of Rawai, said he'd let Reinard know where we were and that he should come to meet us once he'd scoured for someone who could speak Thai, English and the native language of those remote islanders whose story we had been brought together for. With a wave from the car window, Gitano left us standing.

'Not exactly to plan,' said Jake mechanically, a little dazed.

I shook my head. 'I guess when a random guy emails out of the blue and tells you he wants to make a documentary about indigenous wisdom, you've got to suspend normal expectations.'

Jake looked up and down the street, sat down on a hardened plastic case containing some of his equipment and then, as I was giving up on a response, he looked at me again, said simply, 'Quite'.

We waited together in silence as motorbikes passed by. Across the road a few women in short skirts and heels shot pool in a bar, leaning low over their cues and making eyes at passing men. Jake sat bolt upright in a posture oddly perfect, large arms folded and held close to his body, the lights of the street reflecting in his glasses. I wondered if we were about to say anything to one another, begin a conversation, or if there was no need.

'Did you sleep at all on the plane?' I asked after a while.

'No.' He shot back, looking at me momentarily and then away again. I waited, wondering if he might return the question, or some other question.

'I don't like to sleep in public places.'

And with that, in silence, we went on sitting.

After a while, with no sight or word from the man we knew only from email, I made my excuses and said I was going for a walk. The town was quiet, a mixture of cheap-looking cocktail bars and attempts at British pubs; none of the hedonism that was wrapped along beaches further round the coast. Passing by the busier establishments, I came to a place with short wooden tables and chairs outside, where a plastic banner with photos of food was hanging between two trestles, and on top of which some planks of wood held the burners and large woks of a basic kitchen.

Groups of backpackers dominated most of the tables, poring over guidebooks and smartphones. Off to one side, at an almost empty table, a man sat silent and alone. Older than most of the crowd, he was nevertheless dressed in the same style: long shorts and a loose shirt opened low to the chest, with Buddhist symbols woven into its fabric. From his chin grew a large, wiry beard, with stripes of grey growing in it at either side of his mouth. He sat over a bowl of noodles, steam flushing his face, and as I pulled up one of the remaining stools, a little further down the table, two keen blue eyes stared at me. He leant closer.

'I'm Andy the Philosopher,' said a Northumberland accent as Andy pulled his seat in to the table and stuck out a hand. 'Nice to meet you.'

He looked at me from over the bowl of noodles. There was a harmless but uncomfortable intensity to him. Tiny white dots of three cysts grew like small anthills from the wet, pink tissue on the cusp of one eyelid.

'What brings you to Phuket?' asked Andy.

'Just work. You?'

'I'm travelling,' replied Andy, boldly delivering that single word, so functional and yet loaded with whatever meaning we wished to invest in it.

'And you're a philosopher?'

'I help people understand their life; their mind, their body.'

And at that, Andy stood up and, without warning, pulled down the waistband of his shorts. He pointed to his hip. Aside from having revealed the long cleft of his leg turning shadowy on its way into groin, and the hairy edge of his pubis, there was a large, dark brown scar. I looked at round circles where flesh had been pulled open and grown back in a wrinkling weave of cicatrised skin.

'I'm healing,' announced Andy.

I leant back, got comfortable, left the conversation to him; the words were queuing up in his mouth, hours end-to-end. The guy wanted to talk.

'I was born with a bent skeleton,' he said and lifted his shirt, showed more of the same torn and then stitched skin extending up his side. 'The doctors inserted rods and bolts, they tightened the bolts to pull me straight. That was until I was eleven. From eleven to sixteen' – Andy wound a two-handed corkscrew in the air – 'I had to tighten them meself.'

Why Andy was sitting alone wasn't much of a mystery. His eyes kept on straight at me, snagging with each blink as the lids brushed the cysts and surface of his eyeballs. I sat listening while around us rang the clatter of bowls being cleared from tables and washed in buckets in a small kitchen.

'And now the man you see' – he spread his arms – 'is healthier than I ever expected to be.'

I smiled, happy for him. Scars to prove it, a bit forward, but no doubting it was too strange and oddly personal a confessional to be anything but truth.

'That's a great thing.'

'Thank you,' he gave a small bow of acknowledgment. 'Now I'm using that story to help people change their lives.'

'How's that going?'

'It's working.' Andy puffed up. 'I can hold people's attention in a way others can't. Thousands of people. When I speak,' he paused, closed softly, 'people listen.'

He was losing me, my ears tuning out of their own accord.

'What's your secret?'

'It's just … Me. The experiences I've had inside this body mean I can reach entire crowds with my words.'

His crowd of one wasn't convinced, but I heard him out.

'Things make sense to me in a way they don't to other people. I can offer whole new understandings of the world.' Ever so slightly, he checked himself. 'I'm not a messiah.'

With that much I agreed.

'But there's something, similar.'

I blew out a puff of air, vibrating on my lips. Losing patience.

'You don't think that maybe, even with the disabilities you've overcome, it's a bit arrogant to value your own experience of life so highly above everyone else's? I mean, everyone has their own story.'

Andy buckled slightly at the challenge, mine perhaps the first pushback he'd received from the New Age wanderers and assorted hedonists washing up all round South East Asia.

'It's not that it's more valuable.' He leant in, his bowl of noodles now only water with green and red chilli, slices of spring onion floating. 'But it offers them an understanding that most people can't have without meeting me.'

I looked up and down the beach for a get-out. Nothing doing. Andy pushed the bowl aside; just the two of us.

'When people realise the way I've healed myself, it can change them.'

In his words were no hint of doubt, the man a missionary for his own order.

'So why did you come to Thailand to change people? Why not at home, where you can talk to everyone, not just tourists?'

It was perhaps a little direct, but those were the terms he'd put us on.

'What I'm doing,' Andy swallowed hard, 'has taken a real commitment.'

I backed out of confrontation then. In a moment, Andy's tone shifted; defensiveness sprung up and, regular as ever, ego proved only the most faithful marker of vulnerability. Whatever his bluster, the guy needed compassion.

'I'm putting my faith in myself and in the world.'

'In what way?'

'Well, it's a big thing I've decided here … cutting all my ties with Britain.'

'Why have you done that?'

Andy looked straight at me. 'I can't live there. And I'm sorry, but I have to tell people I meet about the battle I had to fix my body, otherwise they think I'm fine.'

'That's fair enough. I don't mind you telling me about it.'

Andy gave a nod of thanks. 'I need massages for my body. Almost every day, and here I can just about afford that, but at home I can't ever manage the costs of enough physiotherapy.'

I shuffled in my seat as Andy got honest, went beyond his self-perception and instead just told me his real story, behind the legend, who he was.

'My house … I can't afford to keep it warm, and if it's cold then my bones hurt too much.' He shrugged. 'So the climate here is easier.'

'But you receive benefits to help?'

'For another seven weeks,' Andy looked at me, fragile but determined. 'Then they stop.'

'They weren't enough to survive on? To heat your house?'

He shook his head.

'My benefits were cut by the new government, by the Tories. They cut them because I can walk, and I can stand up' – he spread his arms in evidence of his body – 'but I'm not like you. I can't work, because after a couple of hours it hurts. My body starts pulling itself apart, and after a couple of hours the pain is too much.'

His face glowered, defensive, as if he had to make the point again, and at the same time was tired of making it.

'When they assess me on the phone, they ask if I can stand, and if I tell them that I can they say it's fine, I can work, and I should tell them about it when I can't.'

That was quite the tragedy; turned out 'first-world problems' weren't all so trivial after all. Despite his claim to the contrary, he didn't seem so natural a storyteller; he misread his listener, was too ardent about himself when I was sceptical, turned self-conscious when I became sympathetic. There was an earnestness in him of someone who has spent a long time alone, and who carries a burden.

The sounds of washing-up mingled with cicadas. I interrupted our silence.

'And what if it doesn't work out here?'

He shook his head, defiantly resigned. 'I've left my mum with an account that has enough money to fly me home from anywhere on the planet. Or I might make my way to India, if Thailand doesn't go all right. The culture there will take care of me; I know that I can go and live with the monks, I can find a temple that will take me.' He looked over, self-aware, momentarily. 'As a white man and a cripple, I know that in India I'll get a lot of respect.'

Damn. In that instant I heard the sound of Western society, like a boulder dropping slow but powerful, down through the deep sea, and finally nestling with a white puff of sand to hit rock bottom. Buddhist monks and Hindu hermits, prompted by white skin, were going to step in for the welfare state. Humanity in the Western world was a thing of the past, we could no longer afford it; taking care of the disabled was now a luxury, and small wonder the kids were all in Thailand so desperately seeking out oblivion. Andy interrupted my thoughts with a loud sigh.

'And if that doesn't work, and I go home' – Andy straightened in his delivery, proudly Northern and dour as his voice reached up – 'then I know a big bridge I can jump off.' He clenched his fist in determination. 'I'm not afraid to die by my own hand.'

'Bloody hell, Andy!' Our acquaintance only ten minutes old

and Andy having shared both his groin and a suicide oath with me. 'Don't worry … it's not going to come to that!'

I reached for his forearm, gave it a squeeze. We looked at one another. Andy just as intense, his small mouth shut tight and surrounded by its straggly beard. He had such an innocent face; those blue eyes, slightly afraid but resolute that he would give his utmost to being brave.

'It won't come to that,' I repeated, giving a calmer smile. But what did I know?

Let's Go Shoot a Film! – night

It was late when I made my way back to where Jake still waited at Rawai Pier. As I walked I saw the flowers I'd once delivered to London offices, their stems cut and stuck in vases, but now growing wild at the roadside. Birds of paradise came screeching blue from out the beaks of their orange bud, heliconias burned in bright red torches from the undergrowth. A little pagoda stood at the edge of a promenade where the roof tiles, along with one of the supporting columns, had caved in and slipped down into the sea, so that mangled rebar burst out of the concrete and waved from the surface of the water like an industrial seaweed.

Jake and I nodded new greetings at one another, silent for a moment.

'Any news?' I asked.

'I just got a message. He said five minutes.'

Ten passed before, at the entrance of the rundown village, a man appeared. It was only a silhouette that moved towards us, with his hand on his hip and seeming to clasp his forehead as the detail of the figure came clearer into view. He wore a short-sleeved shirt, shorts past his knees and sturdy sandals. He was long-legged, long-armed and with a gangly, European gait. It was him for sure, Reinard ... the Luxembourger. He emerged from out of the high gateposts of the village, lifting his arm in a languid wave. And we were under way.

'Well, would you look at this.' We all embraced in polite hugs. 'Who'd have thought it was really going to happen?'

Let's get things straight from the outset: Reinard was a good guy. Gitano was right, the man had a good heart, the best of hearts ... that was part of the problem and probably how he came to drive me so spare, because deep down, I liked him all along. I wanted to help, felt responsible for doing what I could to make good on his hare-brained dreams. It's harder to wash your hands of the good guys, to just stand aside and let them sink. Reinard folded his arms, stepping back as if to admire me and Jake, real specimens and the twin keys to his media destiny. That was one of the things that had always given away how modest the man was in his capabilities; the fact he thought me and Jake were big-time, were gonna bring it all together for him.

We looked one another up and down. Reinard couldn't stop grinning … his big white teeth reflected bright in the glow of the street lamps. His hair was fair, blue eyes but dark black eyelashes, proper Aryan, high cheekbones and a pointed chin. Jake stood next to me with ten thousand pounds of recording technology strapped to his back: built like a gorilla, a real silverback, Jake had spent hours of life holding heavy cameras at unnatural angles until his arms had grown Spartan. Reinard put his hands on his hips, down to business.

'Now I don't want you to panic …'

Thirty seconds in, standing on a derelict pier in Thailand, and already Reinard was talking panic: 'But the translators from Bangkok can't be here. I was at the sea gypsy village just now, trying to estab-lish if someone else could help.'

He had that quirky accent, straight-laced Germanic, honest but with a slight quiver, a sing-song to his words, lots of affirmations. *'Ja, you know?', 'Right-right … alles ist klar?'* were all interspersed peri-odically to check you were still aboard his train of thought. I would come to realise that Luxembourg, its bankers, suburbs and wealth per capita, was a large part of what had taken us there. Reinard was a refugee from capital; the man's spirit had compelled him to seek out the world's curiosities, sent him looking for some respite from the tidy land of modernity and finance that he'd known growing up in the Grand Duchy. We stood in the street listening to him talk. I suppose we must've said a few things in return, not much, it all turned dreamlike in the dim night and confusion of arrival.

'It was OK with Gitano? The drive?'

'Apart from his driving,' said Jake.

'Ahh, I'm sorry about that. He's a good person, I like to give him work when I can. He used to be a famous juggler, a high-speed juggler at the Kremlin, performed with Rostropovich ... but lately, he drinks too much.'

'Yeah. He said he was getting back in training.'

'He always says that.'

We made our way down the pier, walking beneath the occasional zip of a reel as a line was cast out by a fisherman. Boats bobbed in the shallows, others pulled right up on to the beach, a light attached to the rear end of each, above the outboard. Light flashed red, flashed green, flashed red. Reinard talked, talked incessantly as Jake interrupted, pointing back over to the collapsed pagoda.

'What happened there? It looks pretty catastrophic, whatever it was.'

'Ah, it was terrible.' Reinard clasped his forehead. 'A couple of tourists were smoking pot, getting high in a car somewhere out of town. They drove back into Rawai, paranoid, scared to death they were being followed. They saw headlights big in the mirror behind them and the guys thought they were destined for police and then, you know, a decade in a Thai jail. They sped down the end of the highway, and hit the pagoda.'

Reinard recreated the collision, hitting his fist with his palm. 'They vaulted into the sea. The girl, she drowned. Her boyfriend, they got him out faster, so they got chance to pump his lungs dry in the hospital.'

He nodded in acknowledgment of the grim story, then waved his hands as if to clear that ominous memory, make space for the magnificent dream of his which we were all set to bring true.

'But tonight, tonight it's a big night. Tonight we meet the crew. And tomorrow we get down to our business here. From tomorrow we are filmmakers, tomorrow we start making movies.'

No matter what happened, Reinard would never lose his appetite for making those announcements; a sense of the monumental was never far from his mind. That was one of the lessons I learned out there. Don't trust *filmmakers*. If people are *making a film*, hear them out, but when someone tells you they're *a filmmaker*, or *making movies*, you can never be sceptical enough.

The water swirled, clouded with mud, lapping at the footings of the pier.

'I have confidence that whatever difficulties come our way, we'll be more than a match for them.'

I didn't like how much he was talking about difficulties. Difficulties and *no-need-to-panic* weren't supposed to have been such early parts of the plan. I watched as Reinard made a phone call, the man exactly as he'd come across over the internet. He had a way about him that did not inspire confidence, but in it also an earnestness; there was a sense of certainty there, one that could carry you along with it, make it hard to say no when he invited you to join his plans by which he felt sure the world could be made a better place.

'Yeah, Laurie. I got the guys, we're ready for you. Thanks,' he smiled. '*Kapong-kap!*'

Reinard put the phone away, looked back at us with those sharp blue eyes. He clapped his hands together. 'So, let's go shoot a film!'

A humming grew gradually louder as a dinghy bounced high and quick over the water. A white-haired man in a white T-shirt came into view, his hand on the tiller of the outboard as the boat skipped over the tops of waves and piloted in to us on an arc, a sickle of white spray foaming out behind and floating away into dark sea. The dinghy came closer, the outboard sputtered, so that eventually you heard the individual bursts of its engine coughing up sea. The man shouted over the noise of the wind and the dinghy rocked, danced up and down on breaking waves. A sharp voice, harsh but not angry, roared through the spray. 'Careful on that pier. It's more slippery than a butcher's dick!'

And that was Laurie.

My rucksack pulled at my shoulders, left me top-heavy with its ballast, unsteady on my feet, water never really my environment before then.

'You want me to load my bag in, or just jump?' I asked.

Laurie shouted, perhaps not directly at me, but nonetheless he shouted, just like I soon learned he shouted at any situation in which people were hesitating and complicating matters. Shouting does not mean the same on a boat as it does on land.

'*Just get in the boat and sit down!*'

We loaded in, four sets of hands grabbing with anxiety at Jake's rucksack, our reason for being here. There was stress in the air, feet slipping on the deck, the dinghy bouncing on the water against the pier. Laurie was trying to hold it away from the pier so that it didn't puncture, trying to hold it to the pier so that it didn't drift.

'Jesus Christ! These fucking barnacles are like razors. They'll cut the Zodiac to shreds. *Reinard! This is a fucking nightmare!*'

We all passed through a curtain of spray and into the boat. Laurie dropped the outboard back in the sea and we sped out towards the schooner that was waiting at anchor.

'And this,' announced Reinard grandly as we went, 'this is our captain. Laurie here will take us aboard the *Atlanta* and out to the island of Surin. Laurie has sailed twice around the world, and with him, I promise you we are in the best hands.'

'Good to meet you, Jake,' said Laurie. 'Good to meet you, Jules.'

Laurie was an older guy, direct and Australian; his entire life had been spent in and out of ports, and meeting new people was to Laurie a thing no more complicated than sticking out a hand for whomever was in front of him to shake. That first hello in the boat was as incidental as if it had taken place while passing anonymously in a street or across beers in a bar, and meeting Laurie did not at first give away any hint at the many treasures of the world he kept inside him. The stories and expertise he had amassed were at odds with the first impression he gave; he was as plain spoken as they come, but over the following days, one after the next, the tales emerged from him.

We motored out over the small waves, perhaps only a few hundred metres back to the boat, the launch stable in the water under the weight of our four bodies and baggage. *Atlanta* waited at anchor, framed perfectly by the Andaman, its high masts needling their silhouettes into a dark sky, criss-crossed by webs of rigging and furled sails strapped to their booms. A couple of portholes in the side of the boat shone like buttons of light, casting yellow puddles on to rippling waves that leapt up with a new wind coming through. The curved body of the schooner rocked calmly on the warm water, where the smell of salt had not yet grown familiar, and still came to me, new and thick.

Atlanta – night

The correspondence that had led me to standing there on the deck of *Atlanta* was, in retrospect, a good indicator of how that week would pan out. Short of money but back then certain a lucky break waited just up ahead, Reinard's introduction of himself, from out of the blue, fitted well enough with the career trajectory I was planning for myself. The logic was rudimentary, little more than a belief that at some point something had to happen that would allow me stop treading financial water. If someone had an interesting idea then I had ears for them … If they were ready to pay me for it, I was theirs.

My involvement was to be blamed specifically on an article I'd written about the politics of an Italian banking crisis, which – typically outspoken, I suppose – had captured Reinard's imagination. Living out in Thailand, going slowly native, Reinard had found the piece and thought it magnificent: incendiary, passionate, exactly the sort of fire his own project needed. From then on, at least until he met me, I was the man for the job. Reinard's mind was made up: he wanted a writer. Whether or not he ever *needed* a writer was another matter, but that sort of consideration never stood in Reinard's way. In him was some half-baked idea, as tender as it was unformed and run-of-the-mill, that we were going to capture the wisdom of indigenous communities and bring back a filmic version of their message to help kill off capitalism and save modern society from itself. The man was even crazier than I was, had been too long out in the sun.

Over a year of contact, Reinard's plans had fluctuated wildly, his stories mostly so tall it was hard to get up close enough to see which parts might actually be true and where the leaps of faith began. One week a multibillion-dollar Swiss corporation would be all set to sponsor the voyage, the next he was detailing how his time with

Cherokee Indians had given him vital experience engaging with remote communities. With Reinard it wasn't deceit, there wasn't a bit of dishonesty in him, but he was so sure of his visions that the endless brush-offs donors tried to give had all gone clear over his head. Every euphemism-laced lack of interest seemed to fill Reinard with a rich optimism. The man's emails read like a fraud scam that wanted to save the world but never requested your card details. One correspondence with me had told of his friend, a diver on offshore oil rigs, who had secured him a meeting with an oil executive keen to fund projects seen to be protecting the rights of indigenous peoples. Another message described a renewable energy investor who 'really means business on climate change and native tribes' and would get behind the project.

As such, in not asking anything from me but seeming to move his ambitions forwards, Reinard had always, tantalisingly, remained just about believable. His funding tactic, he kept assuring me, was always to go in big. Every time, Reinard would ask for a million euros or risk being considered small-time and not taken seriously. I suppose that his determination finally proved contagious, snared me, matched my own conviction that in this life those who are quixotic enough to believe they can change the world are probably obliged to stick together.

When the oil and renewable companies both proved a non-starter, Reinard moved round to finance. He hit up firms who sold insurance to insurance companies, assured us that they had a vested interest in spreading our message and halting climate change so as not to constantly be forking out for major disasters including floods and droughts. What Reinard actually planned to do with any funds he brought in, what they would be spent on, was never so well-developed. Budgets, equipment lists and plans were anathema to him; he was simply determined to change the world and had figured out that if he wanted to make it happen, he'd be sure to need cash.

The funds that had taken us out to Thailand, in the end and rather more modestly, had been stumped up by a US businesswoman, Patty. Another lover of the oceans and sailing, though with more business sense than Reinard, Patty had refurbished a traditional Indonesian sailing boat, hiring a team of local carpenters to build it back from its rotten remains in a mangrove swamp. Naming the vessel *Silolona,* she had fitted it out in boutique styles and high-end furnishings so that its reputation grew steadily, and the thing had since been chartered and visited by the Bushes, Clintons, Blairs and other high-rollers. So it was that she'd been able to oblige when, charmed by Reinard's intent, it came to handing over ten-thousand dollars. To be fair to the man, that pot had been made to go a long way, and Reinard had made promises of more wages for us all, once we had filmed our illustrious pilot film on Surin. He envisaged using this opening episode to convince broadcasters to fund a grand series of global, transoceanic proportions. Standing on the deck of *Atlanta*, none of us knew how far developed the plan might be. All we had was the assurance that it would first involve visiting the mystical-sounding community of a nearby island: those people he told us were known as 'sea gypsies' or, in their own language, the Moken.

The crew itself was a random collection of experience and chance encounter. Reinard brought with him a sound engineer, Erik: a large man from Alabama. He was irrepressibly good-natured but slow, and had recently been made redundant from a renowned French touring circus. Erik had neither his own microphones nor, it slowly became apparent, any real expertise in sound engineering at all, having only been responsible for managing volume levels at the circus, for adjusting sounds rather than recording anything.

Jake, meanwhile – growing up in Berkshire, eager to break out and see the wider world – had some years earlier found his way to Thailand and put his camera experience to good use, making a promotional film for a dog sanctuary. Reinard had stumbled upon that video from where he sat at his desk on the Thai mainland, connected to the world via a modem, and he soon enlisted Jake as his cameraman.

The last of the crew were Laurie and his wife, Nim. Captain of the ship, Laurie was noticeable at first mainly through his wish to keep safe distance from any entanglement other than sailing the boat and sharing stories with those aboard it. *Atlanta* was Laurie's pride and joy, something between his best friend and his child, and he made use of the implicit advantage that there was no doubt the sailing was where his responsibilities both started and stopped. He'd built *Atlanta* himself, in the mid-eighties, working the wood with hand tools and then spending the following decades engaged in the simple pleasure of sailing her around the world.

Nim was a Thai woman half of Laurie's age. Her role – initially to help Laurie run the boat and its galley kitchen – would slowly escalate into one of translating each word of the documentary effort, from production to interview, and every bit of management for which a group of Western men, without a word of Thai but on a boat in Thailand, would eventually rely on her. Heralding from Isaan in the mountains of Thailand's north, Nim spoke broken English, which she used unfailingly to dote on Laurie. She was a country girl through and through, taking enjoyment from the duties of her married life, and the prospect that Laurie loved her as hard as she did him.

I watched the two of them that first night when we were together on the deck, all of us waiting on some word from Reinard. Laurie was perched in his hammock just behind the helm, moving slowly with the rocking of the ship, his feet up on their toes. Beside him, Nim lounged on a mattress as Laurie passed a hairbrush to her out-stretched hand. *'Kapong-kap, Laulie da-ling,'* she said with a large, contented smile. She curled beneath his hammock, combing her black hair, sometimes talking to a mixture of herself and whatever attention Laurie was putting her way. Her jaw stuck forward, chin lifting up with each downward pull of the brush through hair as Nim stared out to sea, illuminated by a lantern and mast light above.

Quietly, perhaps a little confused, we all waited. There was an assumption that Reinard planned to make some sort of address – explain his purposes in more tangible terms and tell us what came next, now that we were all gathered in that place he had worked so hard to bring us to. Not for the last time, the man defied expectations, seeming lost to his thoughts as he paced up and down, watching the water like some vacant admiral, looking out to sea with his arms behind him, one wrist clasped in the other hand. Erik let out a loud yawn and silence lingered, everyone uncertain at the wait. Reinard breathed deep, turned back from the sea, and gave a hearty chuckle.

'Well, gentlemen, it is a pleasure to be together at last. We've all been waiting a long time for this moment and we're going to see some amazing things, I know it. But it will be serious work. I don't really want rules on board, but I have to say that we will be running a dry ship. Alcohol can cause big problems in the communities where we will be working, and we will work better without it.'

Reinard waited for his words to settle, a creaking rope from the mast filling the lengthy pause as he turned back to the sea. Jake and I looked at one another, nodding in agreement, our eyes meeting half-awkwardly, waiting for whatever came next, the moment we would at last get down to business. Reinard mumbled a few syllables, seemingly distracted by his own thoughts, prodding at them as if to find those he wished to deliver.

'I have told you about the Moken, but I will say it again so that we are all understood. I went first to the island of Surin ten years ago, and I stayed with the Moken in their community. After the tsunami destroyed the village in 2004, I went back, to help with reconstruction and supplies. The old chief on Surin was my friend; a wise man his people loved, and since his death I have returned only once.

'The Moken, let me tell you clearly, face dangerous times.' Reinard's tone became stern and he raised his palms in an appeal for understanding. 'Oil and gas companies want to drill in their waters. They are nomadic people, they always moved and they come from a time before national borders. But now, conflict and high security between Thailand, Myanmar, Malaysia, Indonesia, other nations too, mean that they are often prevented from travel, harassed for moving between their island families in the way they always did.'

Reinard's face opened as he spoke, feasting on his own words, his forehead and cheeks shining while the eyes receded into deep, dark shadows shielded by brow and eye sockets from that little light of the deck.

'Most important is fishing.' Reinard shook his head, let out a gallows laugh. 'The Moken always fished and traded fish, but now they are not permitted even to catch a small surplus, because all the fishing licences are given to industrial fishing companies. So the indigenous communities who fish sustainably are forbidden to fish, while trawlers go out and catch every fish in the sea. Their nets destroy the life of the ocean. It is like mowing a lawn where the grass doesn't grow, and mowing it and mowing it.' Reinard pointed below. 'So that now, under us, is only sand and mud and broken coral.'

'Fucking criminals,' I heard Laurie mutter to himself as he looked out to sea. Swaying in his hammock, his face was stern, as if he was too relaxed or tired to voice his full support or anger, but nonetheless felt duty-bound to note it.

Reinard held a lengthy pause, found his next words. 'Because the Moken cannot fish, they have to rely on food aid – mainly rice – from the state. They depend on money sent back by Moken relatives on the mainland, and also on tourism. They cannot trade and so they are dependent. They are a proud people, who now have been made only a tourist attraction. This, my friends, brings us to our purpose here.'

Reinard cleared his throat, straightening up so that the deck light caught him full and messianic, framed by rigging and with two fists clenched in determined triumph.

'The name of our project is to be' – again, that pause, profound and pregnant – '*Earth One – In Search of Wisdom*.'

He certainly wasn't holding anything back, couldn't be accused of a lack of ambition.

'Our message, gentlemen, is to be simply this: *Because she's the only one we've got.*'

Reinard's crescendo felt more like plateau, all of us stranded between the peak he'd seemed to aim for and the unremarkable sentimentality of the words. He paused, perhaps expecting one of us to say something. The small dinghy bumped on the hull below, the deck whispered at the movement of the waves. Erik obliged, finishing a cigarette and leaning on the rigging.

'Sounds like a plan.'

I looked quizzically at the large man from the South. In truth, it didn't sound much at all like a plan, scarcely even the beginnings of one. With the clock already ticking on the week, Reinard had not yet mentioned what exactly the project would involve. Apart from some search for wisdom, there was nothing of itinerary, travel logistics or filming ... but that was besides the point, more grandeur was coming.

Reinard stuck out a finger, lancing an idea as his tone sharpened. 'With this film complete, we will get more funding. I know a carpenter in Hawaii. He is a great craftsman.' Reinard looked up at the stars for compassion. 'And it is such a shame that he drinks so much, but he will make us a traditional Hawaiian canoe. For six people.'

Here came the apogee of all his dreaming. 'It will be made from mahogany, using hand tools, in Honolulu.' His voice quivered with emotion. 'And we will use it to paddle across the Pacific Ring of Fire, as a team, with a marine research vessel in support. From there, we will talk by satellite to the world ... to Bangkok, New York, London, Berlin ... and we will show them the wisdom we have found and the message we want the people of the world to receive.'

Silence hung. Nobody knew what to say. Laurie in his hammock looked over a little sceptical, perhaps, but he kept it to himself. Erik, breaking the silence again, put his large bear paws together and clapped applause. '*All right!*' he boomed with unnerving enthusiasm, full-American in his optimism. From where I stood, paddling the Pacific with this lot remained something I was not so sure about. I had no idea what I was supposed to write about the trip, and still less inclination of our precise message other than a vague wish that the world should not be as it was. I had no doubt that if all human society were made up of Reinards, things would've worked fine with such good intentions alone. As it was, they were not, and so he was condemned to sounding ever so slightly delusional.

Compelled to say something a little more constructive, I stammered. 'That all sounds great, but what's the actual plan? I mean, for this week? We don't have long out here. Do you have an idea of what material you want to get, the main questions you want to ask people, or the narrative for the film?'

Jake turned to me, then back to Reinard, an expression of agreement on his face, like he too felt an answer to the question would not be unhelpful.

Reinard laughed a little, then shook his head. 'This is a Western approach you've brought here. The Moken life will reveal itself to us, and if we go there with plans of what we want to find, we will never understand the wisdom.'

'That's fine,' put in Jake cautiously, 'but you do … have some idea of what you're going to capture, the story you want to tell?'

Reinard gave a chuckle. 'Have faith, have faith. The wisdom will reveal itself, and we go with no preconceptions.'

'You need a plan,' said Jake. 'You always need a plan, something basic, otherwise you end up with nothing that makes any sense.'

Reinard lifted his palms in an appeal for calm, preacher-style, asking that his faith be shared. There could be no room for doubt. Jake and I looked at one another, said nothing. Isolated as Reinard was, out in Thailand the man's main problem – among a number of auxiliary ones yet to be revealed – was an inability to realise that back home, caring so much had gone right out of fashion … imagining the world different to the way it was, a rare talent. Pity for the less fortunate was everywhere; acting on it with some generosity, a donation of money, was noble even. But his surety that you could change the way of thinking of an entire population, of whole nations, was overcooked to say the least. Reinard had lost touch with the fact that, back home in the West, people's minds were made up that the system worked. Surin was so far away from daily life that people didn't feel a need to know about it as anything more than good television.

Even then, it was conspicuous that Reinard had done nothing but repeat things he had already told me in writing, and a little I had learned from some additional reading about the Moken. For all his intensity of feeling, what I'd expected to start taking shape, and what remained notable by its absence, was the beginnings of the plan that Erik had somehow detected. The deck of *Atlanta* bobbed on the waters off Rawai, as if shaking her head.

Papayas – Wednesday, midnight

Reinard turned in soon after his speech, giving a wave as he disappeared below deck. For he and Erik, there would be an early start next morning; the plan being to return to shore and find a translator at the Moken settlement on the edge of Rawai. Jake and I peered over the edge of the boat into the waters of the Andaman as Erik paced slowly up to us.

'Not bad work,' Jake said to me, tipping his head towards the picturesque lights of Rawai.

I nodded, and a cable creaked with the push of Erik's weight against it, the man speaking in his relaxed Southern drawl.

'Once Reinard's fixed funding for *Earth One*, we'll all be sorted a while. Money and wages coming in steady for at least a couple of years while we make our way across the Pacific, I'd say. He knows I'm ready to pack a bag and head out there.'

Jake and I both looked at him and smiled. His faith in Reinard's plans was touching but worrying; it revealed that Erik couldn't see the holes in the idea. He didn't seem to grasp how hard it would be to talk a million euros out of anyone, and he hadn't picked up on the lack of direction for what was coming in the following week. If I was still trying to decide my potential allies in reality against fantasy, Erik was ruling himself out.

'You been much on boats?' he asked.

We shook our heads, and his height, already considerable, seemed to grow a further inch. Erik enjoyed the fact that we were around, filling the role of seamen less experienced than he. You felt that his existence on boats was something of an exercise in not being caught out, nautical faking, and rookies like us made for an easy audience.

'You'll enjoy yourselves, just a few things to be aware of.' He grabbed on to the rigging beside him, hooked an arm round it. 'When you're taking a piss, no problem pissing overboard, but make sure you're holding on when you do.' He pointed at the sea. 'Most men found drowned will always have their zipper down. They get caught out by a wave when they're taking a leak. Nobody sees them go in.'

Jake gave a smile, and Erik shot back a glare to suggest it wasn't funny.

'If you do want to take a piss in the toilet' – he pointed down to the half-square-metre room below deck – 'then sit down. Ain't nothing wrong with sitting down to take a piss on a boat ... Save you pissing everywhere. *Constipation.*' Erik wasn't leaving much to chance or imagination. 'You'll get constipated, but that's normal, especially in the heat because you're dehydrated and you don't walk much on board, so there's no movement' – he pointed at his gut – 'down there.'

'Either that or the opposite!' Laurie shouted from along the deck, trailing into contented laughter. He pulled a bucket of water from the sea and started washing cutlery.

Erik smiled and went on with his advice. 'And the best place to sleep, if you're feeling rough, is below deck and as near the middle of the boat as possible. That's where it's most stable. At the extremities, especially up in the bow, is where there's most movement.'

Erik clapped his hands, rubbing them together. 'But you'll have a great time. You'll get it figured out.'

His eyes shone at us, a little beady, through the frames of his spectacles. He rubbed his hands together some more, and in the silence there came the sound of dry skin brushed firm between large palms.

Getting below deck that night, we figured out that Erik's advice had been good all right, rock-solid truth, and he and Reinard not afraid to follow it. Having taken the two central bunks for themselves, they were curled up like babies, low and in the middle of the boat.

Consequently, Jake and I made our way into the bow, where a room narrowed towards the front of the boat. Ahead of us was the small toilet behind its metal door, and two empty bunks tight on top of one another. Beside where we would sleep were the provisions for our trip, bunks crammed with eggs, potatoes, onions and a bag of rice, a couple of bunches of bananas, and a bag full of papaya, at least one of which was already beyond ripe. Its rich smell of sweet, pungent earth filled the close, warm air of the cabin, crawling unpleasantly high into your nostrils before it lodged at the top of your throat and filtered then through every breath.

For Jake and me, perhaps helped by that papaya turning everything queasy, the toilet made good on Laurie's laughed word of warning. There was, no doubting, not a bit of constipation between us; food returned almost immediately and scarcely any different for the night inside. Chilli, coconut, poultry … undisturbed, those meals shot right back out. Within six hours we were both pissing regularly from our assholes, and through the porthole kept ajar, the sound of ongoing troubles would drift up and out to deck and the fresh air right above the toilet. Before we knew even the first thing about the other, Jake and I had heard one another setting off howitzers a half-dozen times a day, had become pretty well attuned to the different pitch of our singing as it fired. Sometimes we'd press past one another in the narrow passage before the toilet, right beside our bunks and somehow nothing the least awkward about it. Eye-height, on the wall of the toilet, opposite the throne, there was a printed notice laminated in plastic, and which went on to become one of *Atlanta*'s most memorable features for me: IF THE TOILET IS BLOCKED, TALK TO THE CHEF.

Fishless – morning

While Erik and Reinard went to scour the shore for a translator from the sea gypsies' village, Laurie stayed aboard. He was already on deck as I ventured up from a light sleep, interrupted now and then by the reek of papaya. From the other end of the boat I watched the old man as he sat peacefully in his hammock, looking out at the water. He leaned forwards, elbows on his knees, bare-chested, arms skinny but with golf balls for biceps.

He always looked the part, the seasoned sailor with a body conditioned by boats. Whenever Laurie heaved on a rope, you would see precisely the exercise that had kept those muscles shoved permanently under the skin of each arm. His collarbones stuck out high: two perfect right-angles of skeleton, canvases of old skin hanging like slouched awnings from which his long neck stuck out straight. A silver chain trailed beneath his chin, and from it a crystal rested at his chest. Waves of white hair were swept back and stood up on his head, and two stone-grey eyes always looked at you with a sparkle. He considered Australia his homeland, but it was the sea that was Laurie's natural habitat. On his forearm was a tattoo of Neptune, an old-fashioned compass was on the ball of one knee, a panther eating a snake on one bicep and, on the other, a small, dancing devil, holding a trident underneath which was written *Hot Stuff*. Its blowpipe and belly bursting through his other knee, a blue whale broke the surface of the sea and leapt up to his thigh. They were all in the roughest of pale Indian inks, old-fashioned tattoos from before the days of precision needles, fading into the dark brown of his leathery hide, soaked as it was with decades of sun.

Making my way down the boat to where the drinking water was stowed, I gestured a hello, apologetic at interrupting a moment of peace. 'You didn't go ashore?'

'No chance. I wouldn't leave *Atlanta* here unless I had to. I don't trust Rawai … there's been boats moored off Phuket that were raided during full light of day.'

'By who?'

'Fishermen, out for easy money.' Laurie gave a quick nod and removed his glasses to look my way. 'In a yacht yer a sitting duck, y'see. They all know you live on there, so you've got yer cash, yer electronics … ahh, hell … some of these fishermen will just come round and raid the lot. They'll turn yer inside out, Jules! Poor bastards, they don't make money from fishing any more. With all the trawlers there's nothing left to be had in the sea, so of course they're gonna come for the easy pickings.' Laurie shook his head mournfully. 'Same with the pirates in Somalia.'

He caught my look.

'Ah, hell yeah, Jules … You got no work, no fish, you got a family to feed, and you see these big boats out at sea in the Gulf of Aden. What else is a man gonna do?'

Laurie leaned forwards from his hammock.

'Burma's got a big problem too. There was a story recently going round, about some Burmese fishermen in Thailand, at a marina in the south. The fishermen had turned robbers, broke into a farang yacht at anchor and took the family belongings. They ransacked the place, but when the wife came home and interrupted them … the poor fuckers panicked, killed her dead, hacked her up and tried to dispose of the body. Blood everywhere for the husband to get home to.'

'They found them?'

'Yeah, they found them. The guys went on the run, took their boat and fled, but everyone knew who they were. Thai police come down hard where dead foreigners are concerned; tourism's the biggest earner in this country. The islands they've changed so much since I came here thirty years ago. The water too, it's got so salty. Fish numbers are right down, so the fishermen they have to head for the city. The mangroves used to clean the water, kept it alive, supplied it with nutrients and renewed it constantly with oxygen … of course all that's been cut right back now. The priorities are so wrong, and that's no different with these Moken we're going to visit either. I'm telling ya, those guys they know the sea better than anyone.' He lifted a finger, calling attention. 'And nobody respects the sea so much as those people either. They live their lives on boats, but now they're not even allowed to fell a single damn tree to make a new one. Meanwhile you've got logging mafia granted all kinds of concessions to cut down jungle all over Thailand. It's a war on the little guy.'

Laurie waved his arm down the seafront, where white crystals shimmered in dried-up watermarks on boats and planks of wood lining the beach. A few trees reached up, dramatic, grasping from the water. Near to the sand plastic banners were draped on a number of the walls beneath a few billboards. Thai symbols were printed on most of them, but others stated simply and in English, FOR SALE.

'All this, it's being bought up by developers, and the sea gypsies don't stand a chance. It's not just about taking the land, either, because with the trees cut down to make way for hotels, like I said, you don't have their roots and the plants that grow on them putting oxygen into the water like they did.'

'It's funny.' I looked overboard. 'It's easy to think the sea is just salty, and that's it.'

'Ah nah, mate, changes all over. The oceans are saltier nearer the equator, because the heat means there are *bill-ions*' – Laurie almost launched the number – 'absolutely billions of gallons evaporating every day. Then you need the rivers too, that makes a difference. Seas like the Mediterranean, the Black Sea, they'll be gone in a few thousand years or you bet they'll have no fish left in them because of all the salt. The Mediterranean only has its small opening on the Atlantic that keeps feeding it, through the Straits of Gibraltar. There aren't any major rivers emptying into it, it'll just keep turning more and more saline.'

Laurie leaned forward on the coach house of the boat and called out to Nim in pretend Thai English.

'Daling ... can you bring me a kap-kap of tea?'

Nim's voice came from below deck. 'OK, da-ling ... give me minute.'

Laurie reached forward at a metal platter, resting on the roof of the galley and captain's quarters where there shone a few orange crescents of sliced papaya, dotted with greyish seeds. He took one for himself then pushed the tray towards me. His teeth rifled along the length of the fruit, mechanically consuming the flesh, finishing the slice, then tossing the rind into the sea. Shoals of fish moved just below us, flickering silver in the sun; now and then a hundred or more tiny bodies breaking the water to land in applause against the surface. The empty skin of the papaya bobbed, orange against aquamarine, and another group of small fish scattered in a perfect circle before returning to nibble at its rind.

'You've got to start each day with fruit.'

Laurie looked at me with a firm stare. He wiped the back of a hand across his mouth, and I ate from my own papaya, its pungent smell filling my nostrils.

'Papaya especially. It's got all your minerals, it primes your stomach for the day, it's good for your brain, it's got your fibre,' and Laurie gave a not very embarrassed chuckle, deep from his throat as he indicated subtly behind himself. 'And that sorts your gut. I'm telling you, Jules ... it's such good stuff, mate.'

Nim's head appeared from below. 'There you go, Laulie.'

Her arm snaked up to deliver a cup of tea with milk as Laurie rifled along another slice of papaya. He thanked her from between the last mouthfuls of fruit, then blew at the cup and sipped his tea. Replacing the cup on the dark wood of *Atlanta*, with all eight fingers he rubbed the moist flesh of the remaining papaya over the skin of his face, leaving small traces of fruit stuck to his forehead. Nim appeared beside him, ate a slice herself, and then did likewise. Laurie sipped at his tea, pointed to me and then to another slice.

'Great for your skin, too. It's a brilliant moisturiser, really protects you from the sun. These guys, especially the Moken, they know how to look after themselves out here. Nobody respects 'em for it, not really.'

'It seems like they have a hard time of it.'

'Ah yeah.' Laurie cast his arm wide along the beachfront. 'All this lot is under threat from the developers, prime real estate it is. That sea gypsy village will be gone in a decade. The Thai king, he likes 'em, the Moken, so he looks after them a bit, and their land, but the king's old and you don't know about the next guy, whoever his heir is. That's why we got our little house where we did. Isn't it, darling?'

Nim nodded as she went on eating papaya.

'We set up on a quiet part of Ko Lanta, with a lot of sea gypsies around us. They get less hassle from developers if you have some farang who own a place too. Those guys they're part of the sea round here, but they're always being pushed around. I wish a few more people would look out for them a bit better.'

There was something straightforward in Laurie's appreciation of the Moken, something more sincere than Reinard's flights of romantic appreciation. He didn't apportion any otherworldly wisdom to them, saw only people who needed to make a life for themselves and who were being denied that right. Reinard got all that, but he needed the mysticism too – he hankered for their rugged way of life. Laurie and I each finished another slice of papaya and rubbed our faces with the rind, leaving little bits of flesh stuck there, but nobody without papaya on their face to judge the other.

Lost in Translation – afternoon

While Laurie relaxed in his hammock, Jake had stowed himself in the sweltering heat below deck and armed himself with a small box of screwdrivers and bolts, a mirror, and some short lengths of metal. He gave me a quick, excited look as I appeared in the middle room of *Atlanta*'s quarters, where Erik and Reinard had taken the bunks the previous night.

'What's that you're working on?' I asked.

Jake didn't look up. 'A new device I've been developing, to attach to the camera, so that the interviewee can look at my face even when I'm behind the lens.'

Jake didn't go in for details, always assumed others understood his mind as well as he did. He cut a funny figure in that small room, a huge man whose body was almost touching each wall simultaneously from where he hunkered over the table. Spectacles slid down his nose, his skin a milk-white pale that had already started to redden with just the short period of late afternoon that had elapsed between the airport terminal and Gitano's car. He was built like a decathlete, with muscles covering every inch of him, and the small screwdriver seemed faintly ridiculous held at the end of his club-like arms.

'Why does the interviewee need to look at you?'

'To put them at ease,' he said seriously, as if the matter was of great urgency, but Jake hadn't the time to explain it. 'I put my head inside this box behind the camera, and then, using the mirrors at 45-degree angles they see my reflection and not just the lens.' He went back to his screwdriver, muttered to himself. 'And then they relax.'

'Smart,' I said. The contraption looked a little like a periscope.

Jake turned his head slowly back to me, a shade perplexed, as if

I'd failed to grasp that what he was doing there was far more than only 'smart'.

'It's essential that the subject is at ease, otherwise we'll never move the fourth wall.' He looked back at his box again, turning a tiny screw as he muttered to himself. 'And without that, film can never change the world.'

I had heard people talking about this 'fourth wall' in abstract terms before, but never with this sort of importance, as if it actually mattered.

'And I suppose that the fourth wall—'

Jake interrupted me quickly, eyes agitated at my wasting his time. 'Is the name given to the limits of film, where the viewer is made aware or stays unaware of the presence of the camera. The fourth wall is where they enter the film themselves.'

I rocked back on to my heels, gave a smile and turned to the steps leading back above deck. I climbed the ladder slowly, reconsidering how much I could count on Jake to remain another voice of reason.

The hours went slowly, as often they would. Now and then I'd pace the deck, climb rigging, sit on a high perch to admire *Atlanta* and watch the nearby land for however long it would take Reinard to return with his translators. A few cars moved along the seafront of Phuket, small and soundless in a place that felt more distant than the few hundred metres that separated us.

Laurie rocked in his hammock and Nim lounged with a fan as I began to appreciate how time passes on a boat. Conscious that there was nowhere left to explore on board, from up in the rigging the extent to which we would be living on top of one another felt eerily apparent. Below on deck I saw round, metal portholes, where the copper of the brass had oxidised green with salt air, the lids propped open on the heavy bolts that fastened them shut during a storm. The curvature of the deck ran with a red-stained wood bleached pale by sun, and a black guard rail skirted atop elegantly shaped uprights, from which a netting hung to prevent items rolling or falling over-board. A couple of golden, smoke-stained pipes with belled hoods protruded from either side of the helm, just above the engine room, and the coach house stood with a line of circular, brass-framed windows in its side. The boat's white sails were all put away and furled to their booms, the rigging angling high up the masts, and on a few raised levels of the deck were coils of rope and additional sails stowed in canvas bags. Proud but ragged, shielded under a frayed sun canopy and with tattered garlands on her bow, *Atlanta* bobbed among the luxury boats of the marina, dressed in sails and visible woodwork that – against their carbon fibre and plastics – left her looking every bit like a pirate ship.

In time, the maroon coverings of the Zodiac boat reappeared and began to grow in size. A figure, crowned in the floppy brim of Erik's sun hat and dark goatee beard, perched over the outboard as Reinard in a blue and yellow baseball cap leaned out of the front with a rope held up from the water. Between them there huddled two splashes of colour, dark brown faces dressed in blouses, one a bright blue and the other vibrant pink. As they all grew closer, I could see a hefty sack with illustrations of a large green duck upon it. The outboard splut-tered to a halt while the momentum of the boat glided up alongside *Atlanta*, Laurie throwing down his rope ladder and Nim getting to her feet to help two women hitch up their long skirts and clamber on to the deck. Reinard waved his hand through 180 degrees, and smiled up at me as I descended the rigging. 'We have our translators!'

Jake's pink head appeared from below deck as Nim bowed respect-fully to the two Moken women. They returned small and nervous bows at this collection of men suddenly surrounding them on this strange vessel, so large and altogether different to the local fishing boats that occasionally beat slowly past, with their propeller chop-ping at the water from its mount on the end of a long pole.

'Gentlemen! This is Moo Hning, and her friend Pho Nau.'

Reinard made the announcement as grand as ever, and Moo

Hning and Pho Nau gave uncomfortable smiles. Pho Nau had teeth stained red by betel, her face old and thin, with its mouth and chin falling like a slender drop from high, wide cheekbones. Moo Hning gave a jolly smile, her pure black hair tied in a bun with strands of silvery white swirling into its knot. They certainly seemed Moken all right, not so Thai at all … but equally they seemed old, traditional-looking, and unlikely translators. Jake was first to take Reinard at his word and trust that the translators would translate, and with a cheerful hello and outstretched hand he greeted them. The old women nodded but stayed silent, leaving Jake to look back at them uncertainly, and then at Reinard.

'So we can all talk in English?'

'No. But in Thai,' came Reinard's triumphant answer. 'They speak perfect Thai.'

Jake looked back, confused. 'But we don't.'

Having greeted Moo Hning and Pho Nau, Nim led the two women by the hands, encouraging them down the side of the boat to where a few cushions lay below Laurie's hammock.

'Yes, that's true, but Nim does.' Nim looked over as Reinard continued. 'We will speak to Nim, who will translate into Thai, and Moo Hning and Pho Nau can communicate to the people on Surin in their own Moken language.'

Reinard spoke as if he'd pulled off a triumph of anthropology. Erik, still standing in the dinghy, and now holding the large sack with the duck on it against his middle, called over. 'Reinard, take this thing off of me.'

The two of them heaved it on to deck, Reinard's thin arms tense with effort as he pulled it up and let it drop heavily.

'What the hell's that?' Laurie craned his eyes.

'It's fertiliser,' Reinard laughed. 'Duck crap.'

'And what are we doing with it?'

'One of the systems I want to put in place on the island is for filtering drinking water.'

'Using duck crap?' Laurie was shaking his head. 'I thought you wanted to make a film?'

'There are some really very simple technologies that I think the people on the island can benefit from, including one I learned about, where you filter water using straw and a fertiliser.'

Laurie had stopped listening, and from the lower rigging I watched him walk impatiently away. Nim spoke happily with Moo Hning as Pho Nau sat quiet and off to one side. Jake, looking sceptical, returned into the shadow below deck.

Shore Leave – afternoon

With Reinard happy that his project was now adequately staffed, Laurie nicknamed Moo Hning and Pho Nau 'the mamas' and duly left them in the care of Nim. As the midday heat grew, Laurie announced that *Atlanta* would set sail late that afternoon, before dusk and just as an unfavourable wind would drop and the tide begin to turn, so helping us on our journey north towards Myanmar. Surin, our ultimate destination, lay just inside the Thai naval border. Prior to leaving, Laurie would first go ashore himself, taking Erik to help carry back supplies of drinking water. He untied the rope that tethered the Zodiac to *Atlanta*'s side, jumping down to where Erik sat among the large, white, five-gallon plastic bottles.

'Do you want some help?' I asked as Laurie made room for himself.

'This big lug should do it, but come ashore if you like.'

Erik laughed quietly, as if grateful just to have been acknowledged. The pull cord of the outboard rattled back against the engine housing as I climbed down, noticing a broken rail around *Atlanta*'s edge. Laurie hit at it with the back of his hand.

'Careful putting your weight on that as you get into the dinghy, it's another damn tu-it that needs repairing.'

'Tu-it?' I asked, jumping in. 'Is that what the part is called?'

Laurie looked over. 'Nah, mate, it's a *round-to-it* … another thing to "get round to".' He laughed, shaking his head. 'You'll always get some big bastard German standing up there and shouting *zis is zee life!* as he jumps into the water and muggins here just has to listen to the thing split!'

The three of us peeled out into the water, towards land, with *Atlanta* receding away from us. Nim and the Moken women were still talking eagerly to one another, and Reinard leaned on the rigging where he looked quietly out to sea, deep in thought.

'You think Nim's OK, looking after Moo Hning and Pho Nau?' I asked.

'All right? Those three'll be gasbagging all night.'

Back on the jetty of the marina, my balance wavered in my head, with the memory of water still in my stationary legs. Erik and Laurie stayed in the boat, set to make off for a point at the far end of the beachfront, where old vessels and engines had been hauled out of the water and beached upon sands here and there stained black with oil.

'See you back here in two hours, Jules, and don't be late.' Laurie knocked the engine into gear, turned the outboard on its pivot and he and Erik sped fast away, the wind pulling their hair flat back on their heads. I walked down the line of creaking timbers, waves washing around the studs of the jetty that gave way to the line of restaurants, cafés and stallholders selling trinkets that made up the seafront of the town.

From the main street, a boxing gym greeted me with the crash of fists on punch bags, a rattling of speedballs and the slap of flesh hitting the decks. Thai on Thai, farang on Thai, men fought freestyle and knuckles smashed at cheekbones. Above the front of the academy a colourful banner, in English, encouraged people to donate money and support those local children growing up on Phuket's streets, helping them take up a training position to teach the life skills and discipline of the fight school. I smiled at the thought of that transfer of Westerners' money, funding the training of those Thai who would then box their ears in drunken bar fights.

In another more cerebral place a chorus of farang laments filled the air as I passed by: 'I wasn't on the right path', 'I'd really lost my way', 'I couldn't find myself back there'. Cafés rang with these reported crises of navigation, as everyone discussed their previously poor sense of spiritual direction. Parts of the beach were like a long, amateur psychiatrist's couch, fashioned from white sand with everyone taking a turn as together they revisited that existential storm they'd left behind. Peace of mind had been waiting for them in a paradise, ruled from a distant capital by despots and junta, but with sun in the sky each morning. Beaches did not count as the real world, sand was a place outside of politics; modern life in the West had driven all those farang to distraction, so that now they needed an island to repair their broken heads. Thailand felt like an adult crèche in the tropics, a sanatorium with coconuts.

At market stalls you saw farang sampling tradition; they haggled with the locals, running them into the ground, in case they were about to be ripped off by the twenty-cents difference, the handful of coppers or dimes they'd earn in five minutes back home. Successfully crushing a local who dared aspire for a better price was just part of fitting in, the threads of a Buddhist wristband were only for show, and back home waited a graduate scheme with a Big Four accountancy firm who'd value the numeracy. Whatever their demeanour with the natives passing in the streets, farang often seemed somehow tense with one another. They dodged eye contact, seldom communicated outside of their own group, and bristled when they came too close in passing. Until they got talking, broke the ice and realised they weren't so bad and probably pretty harmless; deep within, under the skin, you sensed ever so slightly that they rather disliked one another. Each of them pickpocketed the other of their claim to be an individual, an original, and every new white face brought with it the realisation that they were not in fact alone out there. Looking at each other was evidence that what they had done was not as special as they'd been promised, the whole thing only an optimal blend of adventure and international convenience packaged at the right price. All of the photos from back home: the beaches, boats, mountainsides, every last image of Thailand had had the bodies airbrushed out. People had expected solitude, peace of mind, discovery … and then arrived to find they needed a twenty-minute death march down a furnace-hot beach just to get a clear selfie without some Australian's ankle bracelet sticking into edges of the frame.

For those locals concerned that the Western tourist might one day dry up, thankfully, like everywhere else on earth, Chinese were beginning to arrive in force. The Chinese had a tendency to do the same thing as Western tourists, only without the self-conscious desire to seem unique while doing it. Farang would turn photojournalist, capturing a girlfriend as she bargained authentically for a sea shell, or else they went about artistically photographing plates of untouched food. Meanwhile, the Chinese staged their photos more regularly and obviously. They were happy to stand in the centre of the street, smiling like the petty-bourgeois conquerors of disposable income that Sino industrial policy had allowed them to become; there was nothing unassuming about it. Playing at peasantry was something they were glad to have left behind. They walked in large groups led by a flag so that none would get lost; they had no use for individualised escapism, the muddling through, pawing over a guidebook map in the farang's cherished efforts to 'get off the beaten track'. The Chinese did as the farang, only more efficiently, leaving the Westerners to see an extreme version of their own efforts and, just maybe, realise their own cliché.

As I sat with a drink in a busy café, it was the Russians, with their Slavic heart that liked to keep its warmth concealed, who sometimes seemed most peculiar of all. Whereas the British, Australians, Americans and the rest of our ilk knew just how to do apologies and to express thanks so profuse it was as if they'd paid a friend to fetch them lunch, the Russians, with their twentieth-century experience of communism followed by full-blooded and vicious capitalism shoved in by Swiss and US bankers, were operating under the impression that when you paid a service worker for a service you clear owned the worker for the duration. I watched a man roll his eyes and then shout loud at a waiter delivering an incorrect smoothie, anger that no pureed mango could ever have imagined itself causing. Unmarked by either thanks or any gesture of acknowledgment, correct orders were settled to tables as no more than the customer had paid for and expected, as if – in that finance-fuelled melting pot of culture perverted by tourism – the transaction was understood as a temporary serfdom acquired by capital. After passing a few establishments, it was not hard to understand why some Thai had started putting up handwritten signs in shop windows: '*No Ruski!*'

Finally, in a minimalist café where a row of white faces sat behind silver laptops, once again, there in Thailand I'd seen the future ... a place in which Westerners would one day soon be permitted a life free of work. Already liberated from the factories by robots, next up we would be let out of the offices too. A century hence and Westerners would be given a basic income, a government allowance from cradle to grave: the one stipulation being that they had to spend it, and all of it, all over the world. In so doing we would create a super-abundance of data and personalised marketing content that Western corporations would be entitled to mine for a perfect understanding of consumer behaviour, and a global projection of soft power. The hierarchies of the world would be sanitised but left firmly intact: racism would be replaced by tourism, and people would never think ill of the natives with their smatterings of English and fraying clothes, but neither would they ever expect any more from them than the handing over of a coconut, the bringing of correct change, and that they were smiling, always smiling. Native populations would have smartphones and maybe even cars, but only to facilitate them in their ability to keep a track of measly bank balances and collect farang from the airport.

Worst of all, what really smarted, as I made my way back to the jetty, ready to sail off in the name of Reinard's record of indigenous wisdom, was the raw privilege of it. The knowledge that I'd been born the right side of that unavoidable privilege of skin, language, education, presumed wealth, actual power; that I was of greater relevance in this world of people who ought to have been equal.

PART II

VOYAGE

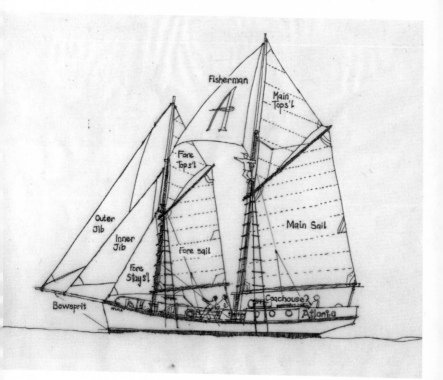

Up Anchor – evening

The heat of afternoon subsided, *Atlanta*'s engine struck up, and Laurie picked through the boats moored at the edge of the marina. Erik dozed below deck and Nim and the Moken women sat cross-legged in conversation as we pulled out into open water, the wind against us and the motor pushing the boat forward in juddering spurts that shook the deck. Laurie muttered and cursed at the head-wind, not really irritably, but in that way I soon learned was his way of ensuring nothing ever really got to him. 'We're burning fuel like it's going out fashion,' he grumbled to anyone within earshot.

The wind would remain unfavourable, but with eight of us on board a boat with only six cramped berths, there was no doubting it was time to leave and gain some sense of momentum. The voyage to Surin would take a full day, and Laurie complained to Reinard about our reliance on the engine and not the sails.

Nim went on talking happily to Moo Hning, calling her 'Mama Moo Hning', while Pho Nau, perhaps the elder of the two, sat more quietly to the side, often seeming to look around suspiciously, her eyes ringed by dark shadows. The deal with the two women, haphaz-ard but straightforward as it was, involved their services of Moken to Thai translation, in return for a voyage to the island. Though Surin was the homeland of both women, the boat journey there – of comfortably more than a hundred miles – was long and risky with the smaller craft of the Moken fishermen, and it was prohibi-tively expensive on a larger boat. The two old women had seized the opportunity for free passage and a first visit to the land of their ancestors. With Nim's English itself far from clear, the situation felt uneasily like Reinard had failed in his efforts to find a translator. Nobody remarked on this, and Jake and I were perhaps the only ones who sensed it at all; the problem was in the past now and new ones waited. We would have to make do.

Sitting on the top of the coach house, I watched Jake appear with a long length of coiled rope, cradled in his arm.

'Laurie, is there somewhere I can move this rope to? It's in the shade where I wanted to sit.'

'Gentlemen! There are no ropes on this boat, only one, and that's the rope that rings the bell.'

Laurie reached out for a grubby length of frayed rope, hanging out of the bottom of a bell oxidising green. He rang it, went on grandly.

'Everything else has a name and a purpose: it is a sheet, a line, a halliard.'

Jake did an about-turn with the not-rope, Laurie ushering him towards an out-of-the way nook. Phuket receded and waters grew around us, the open sea becoming real as bigger waves made the calmness of the marina suddenly apparent. Making our way further from land, a longtail boat, known to the Moken as a *kabang*, came into sight. A lone man was standing in it, his legs spread to balance himself against the pronounced rocking of his small craft. On the rear of the boat a rickety winch was mounted, and his muscular arm pumped hard at a handle, pulling up from the seabed what looked to be lobster cages, some of which were already thrown into the bottom of the *kabang*. Behind the wire, the cages crawled with claws a rusty shade of black, and long, thin tentacles touching at freedom. The man wrestled another cage up from below.

'You're OK?' Laurie shouted overboard, with a raised thumb extended, the man returning it and the two men smiling at one another.

Laurie looked back ahead, saw me watching the Moken man, so small against the wide sea.

'I had to help a few Moken near us on Ko Lanta the other month, take them back ashore on *Atlanta*. Those longtail boats are nimble, but if the waves or tide turns nasty on them, they can get into trouble pretty fast.'

The sun kept on, still hot even in those last hours of daylight, and Laurie disappeared into the galley before coming back above, his hands uncoiling a nylon line wrapped around a block of wood. He fastened the line to the back of the boat and then unravelled it, letting the reel out to sea, where a hook trailed from a metal shape almost like a bent spoon.

'Now, let's see if we can bring us in some fish,' he called happily. The metal caught a little orange sun, imitating light reflecting on the scales of a small fish, and it bounded out behind us with the hope that it would lure the bite of a bigger one.

As we gradually made our way into the Andaman, in the distance appeared a yacht: huge, billionaire-style, with a row of large rotating radars on its bridge. The vessel was high above the water, and with an angular hull that moved through the water on a trajectory that was purposeful but staid compared to the amplified up-and-down movement of *Atlanta* over the waves.

'That thing's enormous,' Erik pointed to the boat through the shimmering heat haze. 'What is it?'

Laurie looked over at the lavish, graceless vessel: designed with the uniformity and sheer sides of a domestic appliance, almost like a fridge floating on the sea. His voice shouted over from behind the wheel, a mixture of disdain and lament.

'Oligarchs, you betchya. That thing will be plugged directly into the New World Order, mate. They'll have radars, satellite link-ups, the lot. They're out on the water, sending back reports on pirates and all the beautiful people of the oceans.'

With a serious expression, Erik nodded, then went on staring at the vessel as, appearing motionless, it moved along the sea. Laurie's words kept on in my head. As the Andaman waves jostled at us, as Moo Hning and Pho Nau prepared to return to their ancestors, the indifference of the super yacht under motor, while *Atlanta* went climbing up and down each wave, had in them the image of two very different existences. One – whatever name it was given, New World Order or otherwise – moved strong but sterile through the sea, while aboard *Atlanta* I looked around and saw colourful blouses and sarongs huddled on a rugged deck, people sharing stories and laughing. On the other side of the coach house, I watched Jake collect the small screws and bolts of his mechanical periscope; he kept the pieces in a tiny jam jar between his crossed legs while he tried to devise a way he could change the world a little.

'Do you come across many of those kind of yachts out here?' I asked.

'You get a few, but not many, and normally only in marinas. Not like in Macau, Hong Kong, Singapore … that's where their kind cluster. They keep to themselves, avoid the likes of us.' Laurie spat a laugh. 'That's not sailing though, Jules. That's just driving around the sea with an engine, and even then they don't do it themselves. Those oligarchs'll have a crew who take care of stuff while they stay below deck.'

Erik remained silent, leaning at the rail with one hand hooked to the rigging. Laurie shook his head a little, eyeing the boat sceptically as it grew smaller in the distance.

'You ever met any of them?'

'Not really. One time I had Steve Fossett on board, you heard of him?'

'The hot air balloonist?'

'That's right, Jules. Real big tycoon too, Steve Fossett. He crashed his balloon in the Pacific and I fished him out.'

I remembered it, his round-the-world race with a British mogul. It seemed so much like another era, a little more innocent; with the super rich still preoccupied by harmless vanities like racing hot air balloons.

'When was that?'

'Twenty years ago, maybe. The Australian coast guard put out an alert over the radio that a balloon was down in the ocean. I was out there, the only boat near enough to get him.'

That was another first. The incidents of Laurie's life that would somehow seem to keep on coming.

'He died, didn't he? A few years ago?'

'Yeah, in a light aircraft, somewhere in the Nevada Desert if I remember right. He just went for the extremes, was flying in a canyon and hit a thermal current that knocked him down and took his engine power. He tried to pull out of it but the guy didn't really know what he was doing.' Laurie looked over at me. 'You ever fly, Jules?'

I shook my head.

'Right, see, when you lose the engine but you've still got altitude, what you have to do is drop the nose and go down at the ground. You pick up speed from your descent, get the engines back, and then pull all the way out. Fossett should've known that, really, but he just opened the throttle all the way up, trying to pull out, so he went into a stall and never got enough altitude to climb out of the canyon. Nobody really knows what happened, but they found the ruin of the plane among the trees. Those canyons they're full of wrecks from that kinda thing.'

'How was it, having him on board?'

Laurie stroked his chin. 'I don't want to speak ill of the dead, but I remember the way he kinda looked around *Atlanta* like he was too good for the place, with his nose in the air. And sure, *Atlanta*'s a bit shabby, but yer know' – Laurie's foghorn laugh sounded a couple of blasts – 'we fished him out the sea! He'd been floating in the water for twelve hours, and we fed him some food, poor bastard. I just gave him some tucker and told him to get some sleep down in the bunks where you and Jake are, but I reckon he thought we might be pirates or summit, out for a ransom. Didn't eat much, like it might be poisoned or some shit, didn't really sleep either, I don't think.'

'And then what, you take him to the nearest port?'

'Nah, mate. Next morning this enormous frigate comes alongside *Atlanta* and lifts him off, HMS something-or-other from the Australian navy. Fuck yeah, Jules, they pull out all the stops for those guys. I think Fossett was glad to be rid of us as soon as he got chance.'

Tuna and Squid – evening

The sunset hit orange on the southern face of each wave, the reverse breaking blue-black with a reflection of dull sky. The sea rolled away from *Atlanta*'s bow and off to the distance, lines of white cresting in a spine of spindrift from their backs. A red-carpeted corridor rolled through the waters with last light, sinking to the sea as the sun shot through a horizon turning purple, and pale trails of cirrus floated in chicanes before setting down to join with the final banks of cloud. The sun lost its bottom third, half, three-quarters, turned red, then crimson, and melted. It tapered, like blown glass sinking, like a hot air balloon crumpling, collapsing to the ocean as clouds screamed after it in shades of white, pink and yellow. With the sun gone, magic lamps let off genies and djinns, and swirling vapours and mists rose up overhead as Laurie looked out to sea from up on the rigging, then called above the sound of wind and wave.

'All right, there's a bit of wind for us. I need some fucking deck apes up here.'

Erik and Reinard took to the mainsail halliards, coming down the mast. Jake and I followed with good intentions as Laurie sized up his makeshift crew.

'All right, on three. One, two ... heave, you motherfuckers! Heave!'

And as the wind picked up and hit the canvas with a crack, we hoisted that first sail, Laurie still shouting over the noise of its wrestle with the wind. 'I said *heave*, you bunch of fucking sissies!'

That sound of *heave!* was bellowed as each of seven sails lifted free, the wind taking each of them for a brief moment, hitting frantically on their fabric until the things were bound and harnessed in place; tied off to trap the invisible engine of the sky's currents. Each of us found our way to their own nook around the deck. Laurie sat back into his hammock behind the wheel, and Erik went down into the galley, where the sound of ice crunched and rattled as he pulled a bag from a cool storage and dropped rocks into glasses. He hummed to himself while a can hissed at the release of its ring pull, and a few slow, deliberate glugs dropped from the neck of a bottle into cups. Deck lights came on above, illuminating a few spots that cast everything outside of it in shade.

'Drinks are served, gentlemen,' Erik called up, and one by one he emerged with gin and tonics for us, the commitment to a dry ship going down with the first sunset. Tiny limes, cut in half and squeezed, floated on the surface, their skins hard and tight, green with patches of yellow, but the juices fresh, sharp, straight from the trees of the island Laurie had recently sailed from.

I leant on the edge of the coach house above the helm. 'How did you get started on all this, Laurie?'

'I was seventeen years old in a jail in New Zealand and reading *On the Road* by this guy called Jack Kerouac, and I thought to myself, "I gotta get my self outta here."'

I smiled.

'You know that book, Jules?'

I nodded as Laurie sipped his drink. It always stayed with me that he asked that. The question was so open and sincere, just like whether I'd ever flown a plane. He never took for granted another's knowledge of the world, and whether by design or nature, he asked everything in a way that ensured there could be no fear of judgement. To Laurie, that book was just another of this world's gems that he'd found for himself, and it was in his nature to want to share that bounty with others. His two touchstones in life were humility and a desire to have fun. Laurie's life upon the open waters often reminded me of those American tramps, cycling the highways for no reason but to be under the stars. They were people called out to the world by the world alone. There was no urge to document or even really to chronicle, just a curiosity for what might wait for them out there. They had none of my, Reinard or Jake's accursed sense of purpose. Laurie looked down into his drink, sucked in his cheeks – a little meek – as if I might've been pondering his admission of time on the inside.

'It was only stupid shit I was in jail for. Burglary and stuff, just for a year … I never hurt anyone; just a bit short of cash and got caught. But it was good for me.'

'How do you mean?'

'It straightened me out, taught me I never wanted to go back. I was lucky I reckon … they sent me to a jail with a big library, and I just spent a year in my cell reading my way through the book trolley every week.'

That sentence took me back to London for a moment, just as the conversation with Andy the Philosopher had, and I realised again how the things that frustrate you at home are never really left behind.

'The government in Britain are planning to ban people receiving books when they're in jail.'

Laurie's eyes gaped; dumbstruck momentarily. 'The fucking cunts. Why would anyone do that?'

The waves broke at *Atlanta*'s side, the sound of Nim's laughter went on, the wind blew. I shrugged sadness that the world was as it was. How was I supposed to know?

'And boats? What took you to boats?'

'Just always worked on the things, I suppose. As a young man I moved to Port Lincoln, south Australia. Got a job on a boat, the good ship *Saint Michael*, pole fishing tuna out at sea.'

'Pole fishing?'

'Yeah, pole fishing,' Laurie stretched his hands way out in front of himself, then clasped them together. 'You'd be in the boat with a great rangoon pole, like a stake held in a harness at your middle, and a rope with a hook on the end. The tuna, they're enormous, mate, and when you get a bite they swim a few strokes before they feel the hook and lift from the water. And that's when you pull!' Laurie lurched back, holding his pretend pole at his middle.

'You'd lift the entire stake and flip the whole tuna out of the water, over your head and into the trawler. You'd have a half dozen men, all lined up around the edges and tossing them back into the hold. The whole deck would be moving and those tuna, mate, they could be up to two metres long. And as you caught them there'd be blood flying everywhere, getting all over everyone.'

Laurie's eyes grew animated, he laughed at his memory as I listened in amazement at that other age to which such a job belonged.

'On top of that, you've already done your chumming, thrown in the chunks of bait to get the tuna biting.' Laurie gestured a wide casting of bait, arm going side to side. 'But that'd bring the sharks, too, when you threw it over, so the boat would be in the middle of a huge feeding frenzy that could knock a small vessel clear into the water. Ahh, it was nasty work, mate ... you'd have guys get hit by another guy's pole, knocked down with the tuna guts. There'd be crew who were blind in one eye where they'd been caught by a hook – ahh yeah, it'll take your eyeball clear out. There were guys falling over under two-metre tuna that would be thrashing on top of them in the hold. The whole boat would become a bloodbath, and if you went overboard once the sharks had arrived, that'd be it.'

Laurie shook his head. 'So many sharks back in the seas then, so many.'

'Are there that many fewer now?'

'You bet, hardly any at all nowadays, they've got no fish left to eat of course. We've fished the ocean to death, mate. I remember going through the straits at Panama, where you see all the tax-dodging bastards with their boats lined up ... all US companies registered to Panama, along with every drug dealer and dictator, you name it, the lot. And I remember when the US fishing companies started bringing in their big boats, and they had helicopters to track the tuna, and had nets to catch them in ... no poles any more.'

Laurie looked at me, like he couldn't believe the future we were sailing for. 'And they caught the lot of it. All the tuna, everything else too. You had the Chilean government, begging the US to stop blocking the cool-water Humboldt Channel, the most bounteous fishery in the world, which let the tuna migrate up Latin America and out to the Pacific. The Chileans were still fishing with poles, and they never stood a chance, the Americans murdered the whole industry with their money. And they took that tuna and fished it so that they could put it in bloody dog food, cat food, in damn fertiliser. They killed the oceans just to make a buck, as is their way.'

Atlanta moved on through the water, sails occasionally relaxing and then pulling taut again. Laurie placed his empty plastic tankard down on the ledge beneath where he leant.

'How come you left tuna fishing?' I asked.

'I had a falling-out with the foreman. I always reckoned the captain of that ship knew I was meant to be at sea. I didn't know it then, but he did, he saw it. He had a second-in-command though, who didn't like me one bit. And one day I was a little bit late and that guy told me to grab my kit and beat it. He sacked me straight out. So I left. The captain was livid when he found out. He got on the phone later that day … said it was a misunderstanding and the job was still mine. But my father, he'd always taught me that when a job's done, it's done. If someone asks you to leave, you don't go back. So I told him "thanks, but no thanks".'

Laurie shrugged a moment, nonchalantly finished up, 'and that advice from my old man, it saved my life.'

'How do you mean?'

'The *Saint Michael* was lost two months later. It went down with all ten men on it.'

'How?'

'It sank.'

'Hit something?'

'Nah, mate. Its weight.' Laurie's eyes bulged as he blew out those two words in answer. 'Those guys would just have been pulling in the tuna, like we always did, and all you see is dollar signs coming in on the end of the poles. Every tuna was worth hundreds of bucks, whole fish that'd be destined for the market in Tokyo, and every Japanese bride knowing she had to have one for any respectable wedding banquet. I know how it would've gone, I can still see it. What we really needed was a shotgun, so you could fire off a shot – loud – to get everyone to stop right away. But the men would've just kept on going even as the weight went over the limit, pulled in too much catch, and once you've passed that critical mass the whole boat is going down, you can't start unloading, it's too late. All ten men lost their lives.' Laurie shook his head. 'Terrible stuff happens out there.'

I sensed then that there was something more than just that chance first job that had taken Laurie out to sea. But I left it at that, guessed that it would come out in its own time.

The falling sun pulled up the moon to the sound of *Atlanta*'s creaking deck. In a shade of mucky yellow and then bright white, its trimmed sphere was hoisted high into the sky and around it the gears of the planets spun. Lying on my back, the projector beam of the moonlight rattled into life on the canvas of the sail, with flecks of dark, granular distortion scratching within the image recorded on the reel. The shadows of ropes hung behind the sail all aglow, long tendrils pulsing black on white as the body of an octopus propelled off and away, bubbles trailing after it. The lines straightened in wind that caught the sail and pulled the image taut, so that shadows shifted before my eyes and instead became a spider's web. A pregnant female laboured across the threads of silk, then gave birth in a sudden fray as a dozen smaller spiders scurried out over the sail and exploded at the night. Slackening in the dropping wind, the canvas folded, took up pleats and became the swirling dress of a dancing woman. A circle appeared on the mainsail and there emerged a black, silhouetted hoop that slid down over a thread of rope as if a ring held on a chain of jewellery. Beside it was a round, stitched repair over an old hole in the sail, its patch standing proud in shadow against the white, so that the swollen head of an old poppy swung groggily upon the slender stalk of a single rope. I watched as its last petal floated free on a gust, and the seed pod opened in a cascade of new flowers flooding out on tiny parachutes. Overhead, the bright line of three stars that made Orion's belt pointed directly towards the solitary light of Ceres, which glowed at the tip of a tail that ended in the claw of Cancer. A little beyond that there shone the twin stars, incandescent, of Gemini, and as we cut across the waves, new stars rose and set.

Beside the helm, Laurie and Erik named constellations and swapped tricks for identifying them. Happily, they picked out new ones in different corners of the sky, trying to remember those stories that had travelled with them through the human universe and since the time of the Babylonians. Looking up at those stars, with no hope or need for any other communication, the vast intricacies that ancient civilisations had found in a night sky made sense. Without any of our new distractions, a story attached to those white, bright burning holes in the firmament must have been as fine a form of entertainment as any could have wished for. Shooting stars passed back and forth, and to look up at the heavens must then have been the best way to spend the long hours from sundown until dawn, in days before nights and sleep were industrialised as part of the day's work.

Laurie leaned around from behind the helm, a serious expression on his face. He looked at the view, waiting for us on the horizon towards which we sailed.

'Enjoy it while it's calm, gentlemen,' he called out. 'This wind has a storm on it.'

Forward we ploughed as the sea picked up and the sails were lowered once more, dropped out of a wind that caught us in its about-turn. Nim wasted no time taking herself below deck while Moo Hning and Pho Nau resisted her staunch invitations that they should join her in the main quarters of the boat. Politely, they got to their feet and, wrapped in large bedsheets, picked their way to the front of the boat where once more they sat huddled together, exposed to the rising elements. Perhaps it was inevitable, but it still felt so wrong the way those women took it dutifully upon themselves to know their place. In the company of Nim – as the captain's wife – they had felt authorised to sit up at the helm under the cover of what protection *Atlanta* offered, but without her they moved immediately to a place where they would not end up underfoot. The two of them stowed away in a spot where they ran no risk of occupying a place above their station, and so, like all of us except Nim, they crouched downwind in what shelter they could find.

As I watched them I wondered about the hierarchy of their world, awkward at what it probably meant in their eyes to be a white man. It was not that I felt the disparity in status caused them any emotional distress, probably less than it did to me, and to be considered in some way rude for where they chose to sit seemed like it worried them more than a little bad weather. Without formal education, equality was an idea that I suspected had been put into my head and not theirs, and while the Moken women were grateful of benevolence and would have been unhappy at having injury done to them, the idea of knowing their place – exposed as it was to the wind and warm drizzle – was not out of keeping with the hard story of their lives. Moo Hning and Pho Nau had lived in beachfront huts, watching aeroplanes fly in and out, watching tourists thumb through wallets and money belts containing their annual family income … It was I who was quaint, naïve, in my surprise that their understanding of the world's hierarchies – and my place in them – might have been anything but steadfast.

On the night that gathered ahead there began to appear spots of white: stars that had come down to shine out of the water. The

Andaman turned gradually to a single, sheer black dice with glowing dots upon it, let fall to roll out towards the horizon, before climbing back to a sky dotted by more stars similarly bright. Headlong into each new wave we crashed, and the length of that line of lights stretched further into the distance, before we gained on the nearest dot and the bright white became tinged with blue and green. *Atlanta* pressed on, bringing into sight the shapes of many pale blue boats, each surrounded by spans of fluorescent lights, radiating outwards and with a long electrical flex draped between them. On those opposite decks, a few fishermen busied themselves with buckets, their silhouettes black against the colourful reflection from the moving sea. Moo Hning and Pho Nau peered up from their nook, the light heavy on their curious faces. Jake stood beside me, and Reinard hung next to him on the rigging, giving an eager wave.

'What is that?' asked Jake.

'Squid!'

Reinard announced it with delight, the brightness of the fluorescent bulbs catching a madness in his eyes as he cast a hand across the scene.

'Why are they out here at night?'

'You only catch squid at night, because squid are attracted to light.'

Motoring forwards, the line of squid boats continued stretching out before us, each one with the same elaborate web of lighting and electrics draped out from the edges of the boat, the windows of their bridges darkened and few signs of life on deck.

'The light shines down below the waves, and the squid see it and come from all around to get to the boats. One by one, that spiral of lights will be turned off, working inwards, smaller, and every time the squid keep flocking to the light that remains. But it's a trap.'

Reinard looked round excitedly, slipping his fingers over one another and then clasping his hands together.

'There's a net, beneath it all. And eventually the light is shining directly under the boat, creating a tight knot of squid, with their tentacles swarming over one another as the net lifts up out of the water, and – *paow!* – it catches them. All at the same time.'

We kept going. There were perhaps twenty boats out there all told, illuminating the black edges of those clouds that coagulated above us into a storm.

'There are so many,' said Jake

'It's always like that out here,' replied Laurie. 'Every single night. All of them getting the catch to take back to the fish market at Phuket Town tomorrow morning.'

Storm – night

Finally it came at us, or maybe it had been there and waiting, unmoving all along, and we simply sailed into it. Up ahead it howled, louder and louder until no longer was it up ahead at all. The horizon was everywhere, surrounding us on all sides. With nothing but black sea in front, the night sky turned white, sheer white and screaming with the noise of sea. Everything fell into blizzard, a spinning sphere, the world collapsing and us stranded, a few bodies on a wooden deck right in the middle of it all. *Atlanta* span in an eternal pirouette as if she was a plate upon the tip of a stick. The plughole came calling to us, pulling at us. Madness struck waves against our every side, spray lashed at the boat, the rest of the world curved down and away into the distance, the horizon no longer a line drawn lengthways but quite clearly a circle, a noose that ensnares everything and then tightened. Shit, but the world really was round after all. Like a spark plug, again and again the sky fired, tried to catch ignition from the storm and shoot down at earth below.

At last, in a sudden burst, lightning broke cloud and chiaroscuro-*scuro-chiaro-scuro* scorched through sky. The bolts split and spread to find their different ways to the horizon, hung whole seconds in the air, so that all was bright and all was beautiful, day was reclaimed from night and lightning poured illumination into those shadows under the mast, before spilling down off the boat and out into the sea. Within a lens of thick glass I saw us shut, a vortex folding over us, a whirlpool opening as we spin, we spin … it's all gone, us the only thing not yet to disappear down this whirling plughole. It was all over, nothing but us and even that not about to last much longer. A Victorian photographer placed a black cloak over the whole boat, put his head inside, and with a flash and the whiff of gunpowder, we were captured: stranded in an image, frozen in light.

At the front of the boat, I saw the shapes of Reinard and Erik wrestle hopelessly to raise the jib, a small, steadying sail off the front of the bowsprit. As they hauled at a rope, the sail filled momentarily with air, seeming to stabilise and cushion *Atlanta* against the impact of wind and waves. For a matter of minutes it did its job as the two men retreated, but in no time at all their efforts had been swallowed in the storm and the sail flapped loose.

Down near the coach house, Erik held at the rigging beside him, endeavouring to look more assured than he seemed.

'Careful you don't slip there, Erik,' said Laurie. 'The deck round here's like a butcher's dick.'

Jake's head emerged up from where he was hunkered. He opened his mouth in a long pause, then ventured a question.

'Laurie, why's a butcher's dick slippery?'

Laurie looked round, as if trying to understand the question, and then he laughed.

'The Maori wrasse, mate! Won't hold still and it's a helluva nasty fish too, they call it the butcher's dick.'

The boat rocked up, rocked down, rocked up ... it would jump fifty metres off the crest of each wave, crashing down into the sea again, as if it were falling repeatedly off a cliff face, somersaulting headlong against eternity. We rode over the contours of the sea, sailing up and down hillsides made of water on that ever-churning body that always, no matter its movement, had seemed so static from dry land; a given entity that did nothing but wrap around the continents of the earth, those shapes and shades of the globe that, until now, had been the only ones that mattered. Suddenly enraged, refusing point-blank to be taken for granted any longer, the sea hit out at us.

Laurie stood, alert, halfway down the length of the deck, looking at the jib in its sorry state, the helm left to its own devices. In the distance I saw it coming. Erik stiffened too, so it must also have caught his eye. Right angles appeared, high over us, and blacker than the black of the night emerged two tower blocks, built out of the water and pushing forwards through the mist of the spray. Erik put his hands to his mouth, called 'look out!', as Laurie also caught sight of the two boats and ran back down the deck to heave on the helm. He pulled the handles round, one after the next, their wooden forms rattling at one another in alarm.

'Fucking pair trawlers!' he snapped out, *Atlanta* veering off to one side as the old Australian stormed to the far rail and climbed up the rigging. He shook a fist at the indifferent metal hull of the industrial boats as they disappeared back towards Phuket.

'The law of the damn sea ... you bastards! You can't cut across another vessel!' Laurie returned to the helm, pushing by me. 'Did you see that, Jules? No damn respect, these big fucking boats. We're a sail boat, we've got right of way out here.'

'I thought we were going through the middle of them.'

Laurie looked at me, a little in shock but nodding terrified agreement. 'You betchya we were! But those were pair trawlers, mate. Those things will sail up to five hundred metres apart, pulling a giant net and catching everything between them, killing the ocean.'

'So that was close?'

Laurie laughed. 'I've had closer.'

As he stepped back and surveyed the scene, *Atlanta* banked up high, real high; she lurched round and stuck straight out of the water before plunging back down to send waves rushing through the alley on the lower side of the boat, the whole length of her deck dunking in and out of the drink like a flood-swollen gutter. That was when Moo Hning and Pho Nau started to scream. I let them scream for me too ... I kept shtum, but I didn't feel any more composed than them. The Andaman was in charge of us and against that frantic movement Laurie appeared from the helm and made his way impatiently up to the bow. Hauling the two petrified Moken to their feet and lifting them up in his arms, he marched them back down the deck.

'Come on, mamas, let's get you out of the weather.' He escorted them to the steps at the entrance to his own quarters, shouted down. 'Nim, come here and help get the mamas into the dry, will ya?'

At that moment my only certainty, as would always prove to be the case on a boat with Laurie, was the fact that he knew exactly what he was doing. As far as I was concerned, in all of my own faculties of reason, we were done for – he'd sailed us into more than we'd bargained for. I watched him march back up the boat, and damn but if Laurie wasn't just as in his element on *Atlanta* as any Moken would prove beneath the sea. His sense of purpose defied his age, defied any age, and he strode, planting each footstep, without thought of a steadying hand on the rigging or a rail. Laurie strolled back up to the bow like the thing were only the wide, flat pavement of a suburban town experiencing mild drizzle.

On a boat you realise that, on land, our consciousness rests primarily in the head and seldom in the body. Terrain, dry and solid, enables this complacency, and the mind can dominate because the earth is a reliable constant beneath it. On water, however, consciousness moves quickly down into the feet. Less glamorous than the mind, feet plant to the deck, and must move quickly and with purpose when whatever is beneath them shifts or sways, as it invariably will. Your foot goes from having something solid under it to a feeling that it is hovering in mid-air, and without you having moved a muscle. Laurie's feet were sharp, were quick … it was as if they had bare-soled crampons on them, each stuck down fast to whatever was under it, like a tent peg hit with a mallet into soft earth. Even if the target was moving, still the foot struck home, and once it was there it would not budge, the thing planted by a weight beyond that of his slight form.

I watched as he climbed to the end of the boat, where the jib had failed in keeping us stable and was now flapping like some forlorn handkerchief preparing to wave us all goodbye forever. With knees and elbows perpendicular to his body, and *Atlanta* still up and down without abatement, Laurie pulled himself up until he was hanging off the end of the boat. The man was old enough to be receiving a full state pension and there he was, two metres off the front, with his white hair and Thai fisherman pants blowing in the gale as the jaws of the ocean went snapping at him. The boat went sinking up, sinking down, sinking up, sinking down. He wrestled the jib, wrestled at that flailing sail as if disciplining a poorly behaved spirit, a mischievous ghost that thrashed on in front of him. Laurie pulled at it, snatched it back from the determined hand of the wind with a cry. 'Get here, you fucker!' he hollered at the abyss, as he wrapped a rope around the unruly sail, lashed it down to the bowsprit and, matter of fact, one knot at a time, tied it off. He climbed back to the deck, marched back to his hammock and, calm as you like, reclined back into it.

Finally, after hours of my stomach rising to my chest, my brain and balance bruised from constant motion, the water began to ease again. Weather there was not governed by time; it was not mornings and afternoons and tomorrows, as broadcast updates have now taught us to expect. Time does not exist, it is only the lined paper that guides us through the universe where weather swarms, appearing and disappearing as a creature of space. It is dropped and shunted by pressures and by fronts, and you will pass into it and pass out of it, with the edges of the cloud bringing a lighter rain, and then a lighter breeze. At long last, some hours later, *Atlanta* sailed from the edge of the storm and returned to more hospitable waters.

We stopped for the night in the presence of a thin seam of uninhabited islands that Laurie knew from previous trips. Large white rocks stood over us, looming from the forest, bared like sharpened teeth in a gaping green mouth. Laurie turned out of the open water and we floated slowly into a deep cove. A good spot to call it a day, he announced. The clouds blew over, and as the wind calmed, the night warmed. With our anchor dropped, I jumped from *Atlanta* into the dark, calm sea, the archipelago faint on the horizon, and the trees of the forested island leaning near at hand. The water pulled me in, dark black but warm as I swam down into it, where disturbed phosphorescence glowed green and white against the movement of my hands, pulling me steadily down into its fathoms.

Floating back to the surface, I watched as Mars glowed pale scarlet just under the moon, the star of Antares a softer red to its side; that distant sun burning up the last of its gases as it awaited supernova in a far away solar system. Bats flew out from the undergrowth of the island, moving at the night and swooping down through erratic arcs, at the base of which you could see their silhouettes picking large mosquitoes out of the air. From the rigging near *Atlanta*'s bow, I saw the outlines of Reinard and Erik talking, and as the waves lapped gently at my side and the world spun peacefully below the galaxy, their conversation floated over the water to me. In a calm voice I heard Reinard say, 'I'm not saying that for sure, but the way the buildings collapsed makes no sense to me. The planes exploded, but I'm telling you, jet fuel can't melt steel beams.'

'So the World Trade Center, all of it? You think 9/11 was an inside job?'

I turned my head, floated on my back and watched the stars above. Reinard gave a small laugh and their discussion of conspiracy and the distant world's politics continued, incongruous, as the phosphorescence flickered and the water pulled and pushed me softly at its surface.

Nautical Miles – Thursday, daybreak

The dawn glowed a dirty red, brushed over high cloud stacks worming out of the horizon in vast mounds of cloud. Mist hung just above the water, and as I drifted in and out of sleep on deck, I heard Laurie and Reinard talking beside the helm. Reinard's straight Luxembourg accent somehow betrayed his innocence, that Germanic ring to it that always sounded slightly quaint.

'I mean, sex and drugs together … I personally never tried it.'

My eyes opened slowly at the conversation. Laurie leaned towards him, his elbow rested on the top of the coach house. My eyes closed again as Laurie responded.

'I think some people, they get hooked, but you don't have to snort cocaine to enjoy sex with a woman.'

My head drifted back to a drowsy sleep, stirred by the wholesome sentiment and an affirmation of human intimacy.

'You just take a little, rub it on her clitoris…' My eyes reopened to see Laurie lift his lip right up, sliding a fingertip inside his mouth, '… and you rub a little under the gums, and you're away.'

Reinard stroked his chin, a thoughtful expression on his face. Laurie looked back at him, gave a short fast nod, as if to make sure he'd been understood, as I slipped back to sleep.

Morning pulled up with the kettle boiling to a whistle in the galley, and, holding mugs of tea, we sat on deck. Laurie perched sideways on his hammock, his feet dangling at the deck and Jake leaning beside him. A few of the sails were up, but the engine was also motoring as the wind pushed us on and I wondered how long it would take before the restricted space of a boat would come to feel normal.

'How far to Surin?' Jake asked.

'Not far, mate, perhaps a few hours,' Laurie responded without looking round. 'Maybe a few dozen nautical miles.'

'I always wondered what the difference was between a mile and a nautical mile.'

Laurie sipped his tea. 'About point one-four of a mile.'

Jake and I kept looking at Laurie, as if that didn't explain much.

'A nautical mile is about 0.86 land miles, and three nautical miles makes a league.'

'But why are they different?'

'Because it's 360 degrees round the equator. Nautical miles correspond to Greenwich Mean Time and the hours in the day. Because the distance around the world is less at the poles than at the equator, a nautical mile evens out those differences so that it's the same distance everywhere. To be absolutely accurate,' Laurie went on, orbiting his tea cup with a hand, 'a nautical mile is one minute of latitude as the earth turns on its axis. And a sixtieth of that, a second, is about a hundred feet.'

I looked on, Jake perhaps cottoning on faster than I was. I understood *why* it made sense, just not precisely *how* it made sense; the numbers and variables came again from the world as a constantly moving sphere rather than the static, horizontal planes of land I took as given.

'You can't get nautical miles in the metric system, because the metric system only relates to distance and not to time.' Laurie let off his foghorn, struck by a funny thought. 'And that used to piss Napoleon off no end.'

Laurie, it would soon become apparent, was a genius without an academic cell in his head. Whether talking about nautical miles, the curvature of the planet, degrees and their relation to time, it all made such easy, effortless sense to him that he almost struggled to explain it. When he outlined those things, he was not explaining a theory but a reality; those notions were simply the lie of the world, its numbers and mathematics. It was all out there and Laurie was just telling it like it was, in ways that made sense to his experience of watching time moving across the water of our sphere. That was a key part of it. Though we all of us knew that the world was not flat, for most of us it might as well have been, whereas Laurie had been obliged to engage fully with the fact that it was not only spherical, but that it was also in the orbit of a range of other spheres. His understanding of the boat and water was no different, for he saw the geometry of each rope, with each of which he had a unique relationship. He saw the direction of the wind on the sails above but also on the water that lay ahead. He had the trigonometry of each sail, the tilt of the rudder, the shapes of the rocks, the angles at which they seemed to dive into the water and what that said about how the formation shaped up beneath the sea. Up above he saw the speed of the moon in the orbit of the earth in the orbit of the sun. He knew not to navigate off Mercury because it moved too fast, the merits of a bearing off of Jupiter rather than Mars, or Saturn when you could see it. He knew which stars worked best if the night were dark enough to show them. All nautical learning and history … Galileo, Magellan, Drake and Nelson were locked fast inside his head to be called upon as required, whether for reference or simple adoration of those men who were heroes to him. There was no doubting the man was in his element on water, and I imagined a sudden end of diesel, and heavy crude fuels, with Laurie called upon to retrain sailors and teach satellites to navigate, in order for the world economy to keep moving on high seas and under sail. He would have loved it.

As we continued north towards Surin and the Myanmar naval border just beyond, the mood became brighter and Moo Hning, Pho Nau, and the rest of the crew grew talkative and cheerful at the prospect of landfall on the island. With Nim translating sentences as best she could, and a few of us huddled in the shade at the front of the boat, Moo Hning told stories of childhood. She spoke slowly, a little choked with the emotion, in a voice that had in it a patience perfectly suited to the pace of a story.

'Life was so hard, so hard. When I was a child we had to escape Myanmar. The civil war there destroyed everything on our island, and we had to learn how to live from the sea. We had to learn which sea plants could be eaten, which not, and we had to scavenge for shell creatures of the shore and rock pools. We were always moving, always moving from island to island.' She pulled at the flowery shoulder of her blouse, shook her head in disbelief. 'Always we move to survive. Our clothes we made from plastic sacks, from fertiliser sacks that we had to stitch together. We had pots and pans that were made from old cans of engine oil. We clean them, cut them in half and would use them to cook over fires.'

Nim translated slowly, quietly, and she herself repeated, 'Always doing anything to survive.'

In all the stories, on the boat or waiting up ahead on Surin, I would later realise that I heard only of how Moken 'survived'. Never once did anyone use the simpler word 'lived', so that Moken life seemed to be understood as a progression from one hardship to the next. If I thought that industrial fishing, island property developers or oil companies and their drilling represented a grave injustice, then to the Moken it was only a statement of the world; it was as if they'd have been existentially confused if life had stopped threatening them with their demise, ceased providing subject for more stories of hardship. Nobody had ever looked after them, and aside from maybe a little less warfare to consider, the perils of the modern world were scarcely any different to the dangers of the old. Sure, had the will been there, new technology and methods of organisation could have solved human scarcity a hundred times over since the days of which Moo Hning spoke, but the injustice of that didn't trouble her, and those solutions existed in an abstract world of which the Moken had little knowledge and no access to. Again and again, I would try hard to resist the judgement, which felt so condescending, but politics and rights seemed to be structures that existed in my head, while in theirs lingered only an abiding sense of unfairness, keen but unbegrudged, as if their society derived its very meaning from peril.

Gradually, shapes appeared in the distance, as if great weights had dropped from the sky. The appearance of islands served somehow to straighten out the bloated bulb of the horizon which, out at sea and without perspective, looked somehow more round, swollen.

'Land ho!' Erik called out, a smile on his face.

There was a scuffing of hardened skin on smooth wood as everyone got to their feet, peering over the rail or taking a few steps up the rigging. The backs of the island, and a tail skirting away from it, were breaking clear of the sea, lifting before us to reveal Surin.

Moo Hning grew emotional, large tears welling, shining, as she wiped the back of her hand over her eyes. Nim put a comforting arm around her and the old lady said something quiet in her ear, then looked round to us.

'She said she knew she would come here on a boat. She saw it in a dream.'

A dream of arriving on an island, by boat, did not seem to me like the most remarkable of prophecies, and as I wondered whether I was just a cynic for failing to grant the story the magic its dreamer had perceived, Nim hugged Moo Hning tight around the shoulders. Moo Hning was forty-eight years old, and looked ten years older, but there was always a happiness to her face that gave her a quality of youth untarnished by hardship. She walked to Reinard, took his hands and thanked him, and then to Laurie, giving a little bow, before walking back to Nim, who translated once again.

'She say thank you, she say nobody ever did anything to help her before.'

Reinard gave a little nod, then dismissed it with a smile. I felt a guilt at her gratitude for our act, not wholly generous, as if Moo Hning had learned to be thankful for the smallest fortune.

'I hate to interrupt the moment,' Laurie called over, 'but when do we get close enough to put down anchor?'

Nim turned to Moo Hning and the two exchanged words.

'She know the way,' said Nim, standing beside Moo Hning, who shone bright in the sun with the confident smile of a wisdom that is kept quiet. She pointed in an easterly direction, and Laurie heaved round on the helm.

Reinard shook his head and laughed quietly. 'I should have known,' I heard him whisper to himself, that gentle respect he always had for the ways of the Moken. 'Of course they know the way. This is their homeland.'

The Island – morning

'There's no way I'm taking *Atlanta* through there … it's shallow water and rocks!' shouted Laurie an hour later. 'I'm telling you, this isn't the right way.'

With a series of curses, he brought out a map and lifted the lid on his computer. Nautical charts appeared on the dusty old screen, with a compass and numbers marking depths. Moo Hning looked doubtfully at the island, less sure than at her first sighting. In Thai, she spoke to Nim, the two of them cross-legged next to one another and beside Pho Nau, each in their floral dresses and shawls that glowed with colour against the grey, sun and salt-bleached wood of the deck.

'Maybe she not sure,' Nim translated. 'Maybe Laulie right.'

Laurie pored over the beaten-up computer and a few charts; checking depths and positions as Moo Hning and Pho Nau sat silently at the bow and, eventually, a GPS system and nautical maps guided us back westwards. I sat beside Laurie, watching the programme on his screen as it calibrated to our position. He looked over at me as *Atlanta* settled on to a new course.

'It's a lot easier with that lot than it used to be.'

'What did you do before?'

Laurie stood up and stepped below deck, coming back holding a small pile of old hardback books. With a thud, he let them drop in front of me.

'That's what I went round the world with, depth gauges and what have you for the entire planet.'

The word *planet* had always sounded to me like a superlative; a word used to exaggerate for effect, adding magnitude to facts that were often quite banal. The tallest, richest or fastest thing *in the world*. Describing oceans, however, and suddenly 'planet' sounded like the correct term; it captured the concepts that were relevant and practical. I lifted the heavy cover of the topmost book, which almost creaked on its bound hinge in letting out the smell of old paper; so timeless and placeless that there in the Andaman I could have been in an old library in Leicestershire or a bookshop in London. The book opened to reveal nothing but page after page of numbers, printed in a thin font and set to a grid that covered each spread. They were headed with simple titles: Pacific Ocean, Atlantic Ocean, Indian Ocean, South Antarctic Ocean, a few details besides, and ran in total for thousands of identical-looking pages covering longitude, latitude and other intricacies of the oceans and seas.

'There's four more books like that below,' said Laurie, opening another and turning a few pages as if it were a photo album full of memories.

It killed me to see the love that Laurie had for all of those records, that log of information and the precise knowledge of how to use it. In those numbers was a detailed picture, readily decipherable to him, that he could read with the same clarity with which you read these words now. I hurt a little at the notion that those abilities and learning would die out in perhaps just one more generation. All those skills were on the precipice of extinction, and that was the first time I realised Laurie had been born precisely on the threshold of the future. The variety of the jobs he had worked – fishing tuna on rangoon poles, diving for sea shells – all came from an era before mechanisation. Laurie was a maestro of the physical realm, where human body, technique and practical thought were currencies that could make a man. In a future of artificial intelligence, where human enterprise moved from the body to the intellect and machines were programmed to have skills on our behalf, I did not know how he would fare … but then again, he would never have to find out. Laurie came from an age that had been obliged to learn the mechanical and analogue world, but had also seen the beginning of a modern time in such a way that he could still perceive the romance in those methods he'd grown up with. I imagined how lonely those books would be after Laurie, with nobody to make sense of the language of their numbers, to turn those pages and see meaning rather than digits, still less to adore their intricacy or the labours that had gone into their compilation.

Up ahead, smoke lifted in a lilac haze from two fires, and against the heavy foliage of rainforest and the stripe of a beach, visible as a dusty shade of yellow were the huts, slowly coming into sight, of the Moken village. It was still early in the morning, not so long after the first true light of day, and we looked up from *Atlanta*'s deck to see mountains ~~shrouded in mist~~ filleted by ribs of white cloud that burned thinner before our eyes, and which tore the vision of the island into shards of densest green and crags stone grey. To one side of the sky, the sun rose in pink, as the opposite end of the horizon burned orange, with twists of cloud like paints on a pallet and the tops of the mountain peering through in black. Where the mist cleared on its lower reaches, the rockface spilled forested guts so that the hot morning wind carried to us the pungent, acrid stench of warmed chlorophyll. The monsoon season was just weeks away, right then the hottest time of year, some six months since the last rains had fallen to draw heat from out the rocks, waters, sands and woods. Trees moved side to side, thrumming with cicadas and birds; the forest shook at us and, looming larger, rocked with the racket of a baby's rattle.

New World Order – midday

The excitement of arrival soon subsided into impatience and confusion. Reinard and Erik disappeared below to ready the kit for disembarking, but soon a sound of excited reactions to Jake's collection of cameras came from up the steps. I peered down to see the two men handling lenses, recorders and camera bodies. On deck the rest of us sat, waiting idly and eating fruit. Nim picked at a slice of watermelon in front of her.

'No seeds in this,' she said, pointing at a few flecks of whitish husk, which had none of the rich, jet black seeds that would normally stand proud against the pink of a melon.

Laurie looked over, chewing aggressively at his own slice. 'And you know why that is, darling? That's because the New World Order doesn't want you to grow your own. They modify them to be sterile, so you have to buy 'em from them or starve.'

My melon crunched under my teeth, the juice running to the sides of my lips. That was the second time Laurie had mentioned a New World Order, and it was strange to hear someone who knew this world so well talk with such certainty of an idea that seemed so dubious. It occurred to me how much of his life he must have spent isolated, out of range of all communication, seeing the world but never staying long enough to learn much more of a place than that which was before his eyes, and often with ears the far side of a language barrier. After settling a few years earlier on the island of Ko Lanta, Laurie had an internet connection installed, and he would connect at ports too, so the totality of his news would be those first few pages that either friends had sent him, or regularly visited websites he had chosen to trust.

It wouldn't be the last time that the issue came up in the time we spent together. I didn't believe in a New World Order, not like Laurie did; I didn't believe in a coordinated sect or club that manipulated everything to their advantage. But at the same time, I had read the same news he had about agricultural corporations producing sterile seeds to boost profits and induce the dependency of small farmers who might once have saved seeds to sow themselves. Laurie might have reached the correct answer even if he didn't have the right working out. He had made logical leaps of faith to explain the illogic of scarcity in a world of abundance; the notion that such simple things were to be denied in an age where we knew so much was plentiful and possible. From that honest starting point his conspiracy had grown. And, ultimately, I shared his indignation, and I agreed with him. Did it much matter if the world had been drawn up so unfairly by a dozen men in suits over a single banquet, or by a greater number of executives, politicians and lobbyists over the course of meetings and political summits held behind similarly closed doors?

Whatever my sympathy with his view, I didn't quite know how to respond; like a priest meeting with an unbeliever and discovering we had similar ideas that originated from different places. This time I couldn't help but challenge him.

'I think the world is the way it is by accident more than design, and the interests of the very rich overlap, rather than being a plot.'

Laurie kept ploughing his face into the dark green rind. 'Well fat lotta' good that does us, Jules. What's the difference?'

He had a point.

'Thing is, with this New World Order,' he said and crunched melon, 'it's personal, mate. There's centuries of Darwinian shit and breeding going on with that lot, it's all evolution and biology, like the animal kingdom. It's like when Fossett was around that time, I mean, the guy was like a turtle.'

'A turtle?'

'Yeah, a damn turtle, like you get out on the Galapagos Islands. Turtles don't fight yer see, they just square up and stick their necks right out of their shells to get higher than the other.' He pointed at me. 'And they do that, because you can't get respect from someone you're having to look up at. Fossett and his kind they know that, and so they stand right over you. Don't defend 'em, Jules, those guys don't give a damn about you and me.'

'I'm not arguing with that, of course they don't. I just don't think they're all working together in a coordinated way.'

'They're working to end the sort of freedoms that I grew up with, and it's the same pattern all over the world.'

'But how?'

'Just look at what they're doing with the Muslims, for starters.'

'How do you mean?'

'Bringing in Sharia law, destroying the Australian way of life.'

I looked sceptical.

'Ahh yeah. The Muslims are only a cover for removing all of our freedoms before the corporate takeover, when the elite will come down in a damn solar-powered spacecraft and kill the lot of us.' He waved a hand away. 'I don't know exactly how it happens, but I'm telling you it doesn't work out well for the likes of you and me. The Rockerfellers and the Illuminati. If that lot had let technology progress as it should have then we'd all be OK on this planet. But that guy, I tell you, Rockerfeller' – Laurie listed it slow – 'he's a murderer, and a criminal, and a cunt. The Bushes and the Clintons, those guys did their work as well.'

The Muslim part was the element that troubled me.

'But, coming back to Muslims, lots of my family are Muslims. And there are lots of Muslim ideas in my family's culture. Most Muslims are no more religious than you or me, they just believe in things as casually as British and Australian people believe in Christmas.'

'Look, Jules, I know everyone only wants to look out for their own, but I saw with my own eyes what happened when the Muslims got into Gran Canaria.'

'What happened?'

'They killed it, mate. They made it sterile. The first time I arrived in that port there was music in the street, and there were small bars and cafés and traders selling jewellery. And then I put down at port fifteen years later and rich Muslims from Morocco and North Africa had started coming in and buying it all up. There was nothing left of the artists and the jewellers.'

'But don't you think that's just the power of capital, of money? I mean, in London places are changing and artists and musicians are driven out by people with more money. It just happens to be that people from North Africa are Muslims, the rich and the poor.'

We both crunched on watermelon, Laurie's face motoring left to right along his rind as he shrugged. There is no argument more powerful than personal experience: what one person has seen with their own eyes is a force far greater than a hundred evidences, or contexts to the contrary, in which they are asked simply to have faith.

'It's in Thailand as well, mate! The Muslims coming in here, out to the islands with their *Allahu Akbar* from the mosques and driving out the tolerant Buddhists.'

'But that's money too, with the Saudi royal family exporting their version of Islam here, paying for Wahhabi mosques in poor countries. And the Muslim population in southern Thailand, near the Malaysian border, is always being persecuted by the Thai authorities, same with the Buddhist nationalists in Myanmar. Muslims protest for equal rights and the police beat them, dozens of them in south Thailand were put in a truck and suffocated as they were driven to the jail. They're repressed, brutally, just like they are in the Philippines, in China, in the West.'

'Well you can see why, mate.'

I pulled back from the impasse we were heading for. The idea of Muslims as a foil for government takeover of our lives was new to me, and the weight of that theory in Laurie's mind would resist any fact I could put to it. I changed the subject.

'When do you think you started seeing government as your enemy?'

'Life, Jules! Life'll teach you this stuff no problem, if you're not part of one of their families, and their centuries of networks and favours.'

'But what happened, what made you so sure?'

'Probably back in the sixties, back when I was an abalone diver in Port Lincoln.' Laurie must have seen my face stay blank. 'You know abalone?'

I shook my head.

'It's a sea snail that lives in deep, deep water: worth a fortune on dinner tables from Tokyo to New York because it's hellish dangerous to get to. You have divers suffering the bends down there, and it's found at the same depths as great white sharks so plenty of men end up eaten.'

Laurie cocked a thumb at himself. 'I was one of the pioneer divers that started the industry in South Australia. You put me on the end of a hookah hose, with a compressor pumping air down from the boat, a belt of weights around my middle and in the heyday of the 1960s I could bring in 500 kilos of abalone by the end of a day, and that was shucked weight, outta the shell! Every boat operator knew I was a gun diver but when I came back from sailing around the world, I'd been driven out. They'd brought in size restrictions and you had to land the catch in the shell, so the authorities could police it. By then the New South Wales fisheries register was being filled out in pencil, the industry had taken a hammering, and I tell you, Jules, it was only being inked in depending on who paid what to the bureaucrats. Those bastards wouldn't give me a diver's licence, while other guys who didn't know what the hell they were doing, guys with heart conditions and no experience, they were free to go down there. I knew there was no good reason for them not to give me a diver's licence, so in the end I wrote an open letter titled *It's a paradox.*'

'What did you write?'

'I blew the whistle. The industry needed someone to do it. I called their game. That bunch of fuckers who couldn't dive had got in close with the bureaucrats controlling it. Pioneer divers like me were getting forced out, and I had two daughters to support.'

'How did you do that after they took your diver's licence?'

'I went in at night, some of the time.' Laurie gave a shudder, as if remembering the dangers. 'But mainly I just started growing tomatoes.'

'Tomatoes?'

'Yep ... tomatoes, to sell at the markets in Melbourne.' Laurie winked. 'Tomatoes were big business in Melbourne.'

'And after you became a whistle-blower, about the abalone, what happened?'

'They fucked me. Put out an all-points bulletin on *Atlanta*. Said I was smuggling drugs, bringing heroin into Australia. I had to go on the run, heading all the way out to sea, towards Polynesia.'

'And were you?'

Laurie looked up, brought out of the story with a sense of hurt in his eyes, saddened by my scepticism.

'Abso-*lutely* not. I've smuggled a bit of cannabis now and then, but never heroin. That stuff ruins lives, that's the one thing I agreed with the fucking government about. And on top of that, they said that I had a piece on board. Said I had a handgun with me.'

'And did you?'

Laurie looked at me, a little amazed. 'Are you fucking kidding?'

I retreated from my judgement, from doubting him, gave a half smile of an apology. Laurie laughed, his klaxon of a laugh, a deep note that came out without his mouth having to move.

''Course I fucking did! You don't ever go out to sea unarmed, Jules.'

I laughed. 'Ever had to use it?'

He shook his head, tapping the wood of *Atlanta*. 'No, not so far. One time, early night in the Malacca Straits, over on the Sumatran side, we had two big dugout canoes appeared on each stern quarter of *Atlanta*' – Laurie spread his arms – 'with silhouettes wielding machetes this damn big. I had instant adrenaline pouring through my body and I shouted loudly to my mate to get up on deck, present arms. The guys in the canoes, they saw we had guns and pretty soon they peeled off into the darkness. Another time, though, South America … ah, that was worse … the vibes then were real freaky. It was broad daylight with an unmarked, grey-painted vessel appearing. That thing must have been about 80-feet long: a low-profile wheelhouse, no superstructure, no masts and running a black flag with a line of men at the bow. We were ten miles of the Cartagena coast, Colombia, and that coast, it's known for pirates. They were heading straight for us and it was right in the tropics but I had the coldest shiver down my spine, Jules. There was two of us on board, me and my partner, but her legs wouldn't function for a few seconds as I thrust the pump-action shotgun into her hands. I screamed at her to get on deck and ran to get the semi-automatic assault rifle. I raced up after her to see the pirates at about two to three hundred metres and hell they were closing fast.' Laurie cradled his imaginary firearm, high on his chest. 'I let off a warning shot and then levelled the rifle. I tell you, I was ready to put a round across their bow. We made it real obvious we were armed, and at that, they changed course to starboard, headed back towards the coast.

'So that did it?'

'Oh yeah … that did it all right.'

Now and then a cooler breeze came at us from across the forest that blanketed the island, bringing on it a smell of leaves blown from the rich foliage of the canopy. Readying to leave for shore, Jake and I ate a few bananas, picked from great bunches, all of them perfect in texture and taste. The bananas out there were never more than a short index finger in length, and filled with rows of seeds the size and shape of large glass marbles, shining black.

'How are you feeling about it all?' I asked Jake, who stood with a tiny banana held in one of his large hands.

'It doesn't seem so well organised, but let's wait and see.'

'What are you taking in your pack?'

'A couple of cameras, small ones, so that we don't upset anyone, can get to know people a bit first, before any real filming.'

'Are Reinard and Erik nearly ready down there?'

Jake shrugged, and went on chewing his banana, crunching as he bit.

Going below deck, a thread of light pierced sharp through a porthole, pointing incriminatingly at where Erik and Reinard stood in the cramped space beyond the galley. They leaned towards one another, each of them holding a glass bottle smudged by sweaty fingerprints mixing with sun cream. One bottle was empty and clear, but filling dark brown from the second, which bore a black-white emblem from Tennessee, and was tipped into the mouth of a funnel. Reinard looked over at me, a guilty impression on his face. Erik went on pouring from the bottle of bourbon, holding the funnel and making sure not a drop was spilt.

'This is just a small gift for the Moken,' Reinard said defensively, 'To thank them for their hospitality, as an offering.'

Maybe it wasn't my business to care, but it felt right to say something. 'I read some of the Moken have problems with alcoholism. You said so yourself.'

Reinard smiled, awkward. 'Some do. But it's patronising to say that they can't be trusted with drink. The West is full of people who ruin their lives with drink, but we still let them drink.'

That might have been a fair point, but it was with a dubious sensation that I left them to it, confused at how Reinard could seemingly hold two such contradictory beliefs within such a short space of time.

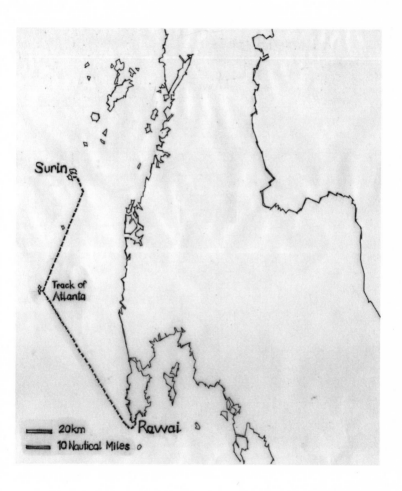

PART III

FILMING

Songkran – dusk

Come the time of our finally setting out across the narrow distance to Surin, the afternoon had grown long and evening was not far away. Dense trees pushed down at the island from the mountains, a line of raised, green palms that appeared to press against the village of bamboo stilt huts, pinning it tight against the sea. It was strange to consider that man so small would more likely push the forest back up the stone mountains, than that a forest so deep and imposing would push man into the sea. Pulling away from the line of trees along the beachfront, a half dozen of the Moken's wooden *kabang* departed the island in a straight formation, with flags of coloured cloth tied and hanging from every bow. One after the next they cut out to sea, their engines with a propeller mounted far behind on the end of a long, metal pole. Water chopped behind them in small explosions of spray, the engine popping a sound of *coppola-coppola-coppola* as the boats delivered their catch of tourists to the same postcard destinations where Moken would once have fished for their livelihoods. With a voice fading into the wind, Laurie shouted from his hammock as the dinghy moved slowly away from the side of *Atlanta*. 'Make sure you get those cameras right in their face, up in the nose. That's how you make a film!'

Reinard waved, gave a thumbs-up as a bubble and tiny wake trailed out behind the outboard motor. The engine laboured to move all seven of us, low through the water, with Moo Hning, Pho Nau and Nim crouched beside the backpack of equipment in the nose of the small boat.

A small gathering of Moken had formed in anticipation of our arrival, having spotted *Atlanta* out at sea. Rolling up trousers or clutching skirts into bunches at the waist, we waded through the shallow waves and on to muddy sands, dragging the dinghy behind. With hugs, Moo Hning greeted those that came to meet us, and then informed us through Nim that she had been told where her relatives lived, that we should find her when we returned to the island the next day.

As she and Pho Nau slipped away, a slight man, dressed in flip-flops and shorts, scrawny compared to the many stouter men of the village, made a path straight for us, nudging others aside to get through. Recognising him as the village chief, Reinard's face lit up. Detecting both Reinard and the bottle in his hand, Chief's face illuminated twice as bright. Both men extended their arms and then Reinard handed him the bottle of bourbon. I watched Chief's eyes shine such a relieved and rapturous delight, as if he had just been presented with an heir to his small island kingdom. For three days straight that was the last anyone saw of Chief. Often I considered that whatever fate awaited the documentary, the one discernible difference we had made in Moken history on Surin was that, for one week in the spring of the early twenty-first century, Chief would never have got so wasted without us.

As interest in the newcomers increased, I walked for a short distance along the front and watched children, half curious and half afraid, as they gathered around the crew upon the shore. Stilt huts made from palm leaves and lengths of bamboo stood on platforms above the slowly incoming tide, which stretched far away down the long beach. Bare-breasted women relaxed in the shade behind huts and partitions of woven palm, nipples pointed towards their stomachs as they sat cross-legged, talking to one another in intense and animated discussion. As I neared, they smiled, and their teeth, stained scarlet by the leaf of the betel they chewed, flashed fast from inside dark lips. An older woman squatted down at the edge of the gathering; her remaining teeth like great cubes of tiny rocks that sat wide and deep inside her gum. Returning my look, she raised a palm wide in a happy greeting and gave a smile that swallowed her eyes into warm, wrinkled puckers.

Once the immediate clamour at our arrival had subsided, I returned to hear Reinard, through Nim, ask one of the Moken to show us where the food for the community was grown. Excited by the responsibility, a teenage boy led us a little way into the jungle; first passing a small clearing from where came the song of water trickling through stone. Pure, cold and clear it ran, slipping over the rockface as Reinard jumped with pleasure, pointing.

'The water supply! This is where we will build the filter.'

Jake and I turned to one another, then back at the clear water, as if both struck by the oddness of a similar thought. Surely, the man was not about to filter the water of a mountain spring, using duck shit? Saying nothing, we went on, and I hoped that the idea would be forgotten.

As the group began moving in separate directions, I followed a path deeper under the cover of trees, along trails that wound and doubled back until all about me were forest gardens. Bushes of chilli plants leaned out of the undergrowth, the chillies like skinny fingers which bled red from the tip, turning orange and then back into the green base around the stalk. Unripe bananas moved green to yellow in the shade of large leaves, and green papaya, splashed with orange, pulled like long, heavy drips falling out of the trunk of their tree. Coconut trees stood high over us in white columns, taller than anything else, and a steady wind pulled through their sharp leaves as if the feathers of a bird in flight. At the very tops, coconuts stuck in the form of burdensome growths, swelling from that nape between leaf and trunk. Groups of hens paced the beach, their claws spread across the sand, and loose red skin wobbling down over the dark, oil-slicked green of their plumage. A flying bug, the size and shape of a bent thumb, hovered above the path, its abdomen trailing out behind like some mid-air refuelling rig. Large wings thrummed loud in humid air as the bug disappeared deep inside the trumpet of a blooming flower, where red veins traced through pale petals and the silhouette of the creature moved against the inner walls of the flower, lit bright by sunlight. From a few isolated spots on the ground, smoke lifted from under sheets of old metal, and pulling the lid aside you saw the just-barely glowing embers of slow-fired wood turning to charcoal for cooking fuel. Butterflies chased one another, a dragonfly docked at the side of a papaya and its red-black body throbbed a beating pulse, base to tip like a fairground ride. On some of the weaker plants, desperate for the rains to come, there were leaves of clawed, serrated edges, beginning to turn inwards on themselves. Yellow lines trickled out of the green, sometimes expanding into dots of bleached light, bursting from the leaf like a flash of heat in an overexposed reel of film.

Every so often a coconut would fall: a cannonball fired quietly to zip through the air and bury itself with a thud into soft sand. Further on, a group of trees stood short and thin with green, diamond-shaped leaves and the eccentric stumps of hairy flowers occasionally blushing full scarlet. From that scarlet shape there formed cloves, figured like short medieval clubs beating with their aroma of spice. Beyond the cloves were nutmeg trees, and moving through the undergrowth a proud cockerel; dressed in white plumage and with a red head that pecked down at bugs along the beach, the bird's tail followed by the shreds of a plastic sack that trailed behind the claw it had snagged. A dog lay on its front, legs out splayed, gnawing frustratedly at a flea-bitten patch of fur stripped back to raw skin. Geckos crawled over rock, occasionally crying a song from their throats, and beyond the palms a small hillside fell away to expose the sheer gradient of the land a little way above. Here you saw the vast height of the trees; their canopy like a parasol on top of polished trunks fifty metres high. Everywhere, from all corners, the chattering of monkeys rang out of trees in a white, incessant noise that soon enough you stopped hearing at all, once the brain had come to understand the sound as only a remarkably loud type of silence. At the edges of the village, fluffy chicks pecked at rubbish among the landfill, smouldering with a light smoke from newly lit piles of wood, cardboard, old clothing and drinks cans burned back to bare alloy, the paint corroding in salt air and the heat of sun and ash. Birds cawed loud, and in the pure white sand, higher up from the damp mud of the lower beach, were black, sun-parched monuments of human stool, sculptures of shit waiting as relics for either history or the next tsunami that would breach the highwater mark. This, garnished with a whiff of smoking plastics, was paradise.

Good fortune proved a better producer than Reinard, and so by chance we had arrived just in time for the Songkran festival with which the Thai marked new year, and which the Moken had adopted as part of a collage of beliefs melding elements of major religion to their deist values about the spiritual life forms found in the sea and the trees. In Thailand they took on Buddhist traditions, while their kin in Malaysia and Indonesia had made use of Islamic ones.

With dusk descending, there came the smell of incense burning, a drum banged loudly, and Reinard called us all to gather at the end of the beach, where a celebration had started up. A man with a chisel chipped wood away from a log shaved of its bark, working it gradually into the shape of a boat. He held the log perpendicular to himself, and with his feet planted either side of it, wedged the thing in position while a circle of woodchip split away and spread all about him. Beside the sculptor a second log, already in the form of a boat, was being painted by children, the light wood disappearing under rich shades of red and green and blue. A third such ornament had small figures placed inside it, tiny human dolls woven from dried palm leaves. Incense was lit, leaving the scent of spice to float across the beachfront in drifts of smoke where the sound of a drum and chanting reverberated. As Moken carried the first ceremonial craft down the beach to the shoreline, Reinard explained that this was where bad omens were placed; the Moken's stories of adversity stowed as spiritual cargo inside each small vessel to be floated out to sea.

At the end of the village, a tightly packed crowd gathered around wicker mats, where a few small cups were filled and refilled from a plastic container of alcohol kept for the occasion. Shots of the opaque white liquid were rifled down from a shared ceramic cup, though the drink was taken only by a small number of elder men and one old woman surrounded by the rest of the community. The sour odour of a rough, cheap spirit rose sharp out of mouths held wide-open, and eyes gaped as the woman finished her dose, violently shaking her head while crying out in a shrill, high-pitched voice that pierced through the veil of drum and smoke. Reinard, standing beside Jake and his camera equipment, smiled with wild excitement in his eyes. That evening I endeavoured to hold back my judgements as I watched Reinard experiment with Jake's cameras, but however hard I tried, however noble I thought the man's ambition, he always struck me as only a film enthusiast recording what he thought were natives. I kept my distance: self-conscious, a little embarrassed, not sure what I was supposed to make of it all, what plan would take shape and what part I'd play if it did. All the while, Reinard spun around himself, looking delightedly at some new enchantment in every direction.

'What a time to arrive. Really, this is perfect. You understand that this is why we had to come here? To the island itself, the heart of the people, their wisdom!'

Jake gave a steady nod, a little less convinced, but nonetheless taking in the scene in all its intensity. A circle of people began to dance at a short distance from us. The man carving out the last of the boats gave a loud grunt of exertion, lowering the dull grey head of his hatchet to wipe sweat from his forehead, droplets forming on the perfect cocoa skin of his forearms and chest. The woman elder, still drinking alcohol, threw back her head and let forth a second loud cry through red-stained teeth, her eyes distant with drink. Reinard, suffering a glee he could not contain, tugged at Jake's arm, urging him to begin filming.

'This, but this is so important to the film! This will show their traditional way of life. I think this has to be an opening scene!'

Reinard trembled with some sense of divine certainty. He slapped a hand to Jake's shoulder who – with seeming reluctance – then knelt to unpack tripods and a couple of small cameras. Reinard took one for himself, following its lens through the crowd, arms outstretched in front of him like some humble pilgrim with a begging bowl for moving images. Jake set up a second camera to record the scene from a distance, and I watched as small red lights blinked on the camera, its gathering footage ready to be reported back to the viewer as our understanding of someone else's tradition. Still trying to get into the spirit of things, I found myself with thoughts of Christmas Days back in Britain, and I wondered if all we were really doing was the equivalent of filming the uncle who every year drinks too much and embarrasses himself with inappropriate behaviour. Were we about to take the Moken version of that annual scene of Songkran, which we had merely chanced upon, and present it as if a representative portrait of a people's daily life? I looked at Reinard, a picture of movie-making contentment and not quite sharing my perception of events. You could see it right then … to him we had struck gold, we had found our authenticity.

Sunken Treasure – Friday, midnight

Below deck the night was hot, with the close air sitting on top of me in that small space beneath the ceiling. Lying on my front, the heat of my chest would trap close between my skin and the gently clinging sheet on the mattress. On my back, parched with thirst and with the papaya still rotting in the next bunk, so much of it was inhaled through my nose the fruit felt like it was re-forming in my mouth. I got up from my bunk and climbed the steps back above deck. Overhead, a small beacon glowed cool green to warn other boats of our position, but aside from the light going in and out, all around was motionless. From down the length of *Atlanta*, a warm brightness lifted out of the coach house, spilling up to the canopy that by day kept the sun from us.

That light was accompanied by a slight, rhythmic tapping, a regular contact of two hard surfaces meeting with a gentle but precise force. I leant beside the large white containers holding our drinking water, took the rope that hung around the neck of one of them, and lowered the heavy bottle so that water splashed into my mug. Stirred by the cooler air, by the water in my mouth, the heat hanging over me dissipated and I walked along the creaking deck. From there, on one side, Nim could be seen, sprawled out sleeping. To the other side, at a short bench, sat Laurie. He crouched forwards into lamplight, and with a small hammer, tapped at a half-circle of shining silver. The black head of the tool was smoothed at its tip, the matt paint knocked away so that it shone in the same bright, keen light as the silver. Under short, fast strikes of the hammer, Laurie held the piece of silver in a set of pliers, his arms manoeuvring around a tiny vice fixed to the side of the bench, where he seemed to be knocking a new shape into the metal. Head lowered, he held his nose close to the object, peering in to examine its curvature. I put my water down, Laurie's head turning towards the sound with the slow calm of someone who, even disturbed at night, knew that within the confines of his boat, the world was safe.

'All right, Jules. You having trouble sleeping?'

'A bit. But it's OK, it's a nice night. You working on something for the boat?'

Laurie shook his head, set down his tools. 'I was just doing a small repair on a piece for a necklace. I used to be a bit of a jeweller, I did, made some stuff to sell, fitted this bench to work at.'

Laurie put the four fingers of one hand down on the bench. Upon the surface were a few slender wires, some gem stones in pouches, and then the forms of different-sized hammers and pliers with long noses for twisting new shapes out of the objects he worked with.

'You've done a lot of different jobs.'

'I wouldn't call many of them "jobs", just stuff to get by most of my life. But yeah. I've farmed a bit, worked as an electrician, taken people out on a lot of boat trips, dived. Dived for all kinds of stuff.'

'You mean pearls, things like that?'

'Not so much pearls. But seafood, like the abalone. Or maintenance work.' Laurie chuckled deep. 'Buried treasure, you name it, I've gone down there for it.'

I looked at him, and though there was the same familiar smile on his face, you could tell that he was perfectly serious.

'Treasure?'

'You betchya. Gold doubloons, pieces of silver, hoards of jewellery, the lot. That was a long time back, mind you.'

'How do you start searching for lost treasure? You look for maps with an X or something?'

Laurie tipped his head, gave a look as if that wasn't quite as crazy a starting-point as it sounded.

'Not exactly, but not far off. I was hired, y'see ... by a British naval historian by the name of Cowan, Rex Cowan. He researched it all, and then sent us down.'

A wind set waves lapping at *Atlanta*'s side.

'Elizabethan clippers, old ships coming back from the colonies, explorers bringing back whatever riches they'd found for the royal families of Europe. Ahh yeah, Cowan found it all. Even right next to Britain. The waters off the Scilly Isles were renowned for sinking ships, damn, those rocks! Cowan would research the naval records, the details of cargo, the old maps. He'd acquire the rights to the wreck from, say, the Dutch government, and in return he'd give them a 25 per cent cut of anything he recovered. Then he'd hire guys like me to go down there, see what we could find, and the team took a share of whatever we brought up.'

Laurie, I came to realise, was as comfortable with breathing apparatus underwater as the rest of us are on land. The place was second-nature to him, and down there he found a delight that set him entirely at ease. Nothing in those depths fazed him because, at root, he was enchanted by it all.

'It was good money?'

'It wasn't bad, for a while. Of course Cowan did all right out of it,' Laurie smiled, 'but then the Treasury figured out just how much money he was making and started taxing him on it, as is their way, of course.'

'You know Britain then, if you were diving by the Scilly Isles?'

'Know it? I was born there. I'm British stock originally. I was born in London, Hampstead, 1943. Slap bang in the middle of World War II. My folks moved out to Australia in 1951, when I was eight, and I've not spent much time over in Britain since. I was back in London, fifteen years ago, my old neighbourhood, up by Parliament Hill.'

I looked around us, the tropical island and the boat, Laurie bare-chested and in his fisherman's pants. I tried to imagine him in the city. Then a thought hit him, he paused and his face marvelled a moment before growing angry.

'I couldn't believe some cunt torched the *Cutty Sark*. Sixteen knots that thing averaged from London to Sydney, the finest ship in any fleet. It only ever lost one race and rumour had it that was with a dirty bottom.'

I raised an eyebrow and he clarified. 'Because of the drag from all the barnacles and shit under it.'

Laurie knew how to wonder at the accuracy of a GPS system, he sometimes watched films streamed over the internet when he was at a marina, he owned a hang-glider with a small propellor and engine on it, controlled by a finger throttle so that he could stay up in the sky for hours. For a man who loved the simplicity of wind and thermal currents, he had no aversion at all to technology, but never did I see him so awestruck with craft or human ingenuity as when he talked of the *Cutty Sark* and its performance in a race from London to Sydney. I smiled, happy with the news I was about to give him.

'They rebuilt it.'

'Huh? Rebuilt it?' he replied, a little confused.

I nodded. 'The *Cutty Sark*, a couple of years ago, it's been fully restored now.'

'Oh. They did?'

I nodded. Laurie seeming a little stumped as the charred timbers of the ship were reconstructed in his understanding of a world he'd left behind. Good news didn't fit with much of how Laurie imagined society panning out. It presented a contrary evidence that perhaps the place wasn't going to the dogs after all. It occurred to me then that the *they* who were, to him, responsible for making sterile seeds and enslaving the people of the world was the same *they*, imprecise and unknown but all-powerful, who had restored the *Cutty Sark*. I wondered how they could be made to fulfil more of that which was good and less that was ill, how it was that they were assumed anonymous in the good that they did but culpable in the bad.

'That's nice to know.' Laurie smiled, giving a definitive nod.

From below deck came a loud noise of sleep, a snore that became a groan, reaching a volume so loud that it must have been Erik. Nim stirred under her single sheet beside us, and all around was dark and still, but for that pool of light where our heads tipped forwards over the wooden box of gemstones and the tools on the bench. The interruption seemed to bring with it a thought, and Laurie stood up. Reaching his arm along the length of a shelf, he searched through its contents, out of sight behind the high lip that stopped things rolling free when weather grew stormy. Laurie's hand guessed its way along the shelf, rummaged, and then lifted out a small, wooden box, fastened by a dirtied bronze clasp and held together by riveted brackets and dovetails at its corners.

'I kept a few pieces of treasure for myself, back in the day.'

He said it as if the thing were a treat of history, maritime confectionery. To the music of a creak of dry hinges, he opened the tiny chest and pulled out a plastic wallet, pressing its sides together so that a small silver coin, dirty with its purity, dropped into his palm.

'This one's a favourite of mine.'

On the coin was a bust, the edges of the thing gnarled so that they may once have been round but were scarcely so any longer, the minted image at its heart well-preserved nevertheless. Laurie pointed at it.

'Alexander the Great. Cowan reckoned that one would've been second century BC. Pure silver.' Laurie handed it over, the thing oddly heavy for its size.

'I'd always wanted to give it as a gift, to one of my daughters.' He rolled his eyes and gave a sigh. 'But I know they wouldn't appreciate its value. They're just like their old man, always short of cash, they'd sell it for a fraction of what it's worth. So I keep it for myself.'

I smiled as I handed the coin back. He gave one of his winks, made a fist with the coin at its heart, and held it to his chest.

A siren hailed loud, shrieking an end to that light sleep; the night still deep and perhaps barely an hour since I'd returned to my bed. *Atlanta* felt as though she was moving, which had not been in anybody's plans until next morning. There came a rattling, frantic beside my head, a rapid clinking and shaking of metal pulled taut. Jake stirred on the bunk below and swung his legs round. Raised voices came from above deck, Laurie calling urgently as he marched to the bow, where the noise of the chain I had heard from my bunk wound tight around the capstan.

'Erik! Get up here, we need your arms!'

And Laurie muttered to himself as he went, 'Idiot, Laurie, you knew that anchor wouldn't hold.'

Jake and I made our way out on to the dark deck as Erik arrived, his feet padding heavily as he rubbed a hand across his face and then put his glasses over his small, tired eyes.

'Is that the anchor drag alarm?'

'Yes it's the damn anchor, the tide's pulling us, I knew it wouldn't hold in that sand.'

The capstan went on turning, hauling up the chain, its links falling into a heap that Laurie then threw into a plastic box.

'The anchor's still down, and pulling underneath us. When it comes up you're going to have to hoist it up and out a bit, away from the boat, and fast.'

Erik lay down on the deck, his large hands and large arms one over the next, pulling at the final section of the chain where it was tethered to a heavy rope. The rattling of the chain accelerated as the anchor came closer, back to the bow and out of the water. Laurie stood right on Erik's shoulder, the man leaning over as he readied to set his large arms to lifting the final metres.

'OK, pull. Get it, fucking get it.'

In that moment Erik's one and only qualification, apart from his obvious size, was an eagerness to help. In all other respects, he was clueless. Laurie looked on, hands pressed at the air between them, seeming to restrain himself out of manners but desperate to take charge. Erik groaned loud, heaved, but he heaved slowly, his cheeks filling with air and face turning red as he lifted. There was something awkwardly encumbered and ineffective about the way he did so, the whole thing somehow resembling a display of effort more than an effort itself. As the man went about slowly moving more rope up on to deck, there came a painful blow and the sound of heavy scraping. One over the other, his hands slogged on, pulling the anchor slowly up, the bill on the end of one metal arm clearly cutting at the bow of *Atlanta*. In an instant, Laurie moved down.

'Get out the fucking way, you're gouging the shit outta the hull.'

Erik leapt up as Laurie leapt down, his arms grabbing at the loosed rope and heaving the thing up, those small but pronounced biceps protruding from each skinny arm. One over the next they came, the rope finished and the anchor, dripping a thin muddy grey soup, dropped on the deck.

With Jake and Reinard beside me, we watched the scene. The rope and chain beside him, Laurie was down on his knees and peering over the edge to inspect any damage visible in the white paint of *Atlanta*. He spoke more gently, as if trying to soothe things.

'Come on, mate, you know you can't do it like that.'

And Erik padded slowly off down the deck, his head down, his feelings hurt; not because he felt Laurie was being unfair, but more because you suspected he knew that he wasn't.

Gasoline Fumes – dawn

Waking up on the mattress I had pulled from the bunk out to the deck, I heard Laurie yawn loudly, then let out the slow, tired groan of a day just starting. There was a cool mist swirling low over the water as he appeared from the coach house. He scratched at his head, looked around him, and I thought how many mornings of his life he had begun exactly in this way. Laurie stumbled sleepy to the edge of the boat; silhouetted against the first light, just a dark grey outline against the pale purples and reds of the sky. He hoisted the leg of the fisherman pants he wore all day and slept in at night, guiding himself with a hand, and a high curve of tinkling piss spouted out of him to slap into the sea. I closed my eyes and rolled over, and as the emptying balloon of his bladder relieved a pressure elsewhere, Laurie let out the loud clap of a fart. I opened my eyes; saw his shadow as he stretched out an arm with a clenched fist and yawned again. His bathroom was the Andaman Sea, his toilet the side of his boat, and yet in so many respects Laurie was identical to middle-aged men all around the world.

Perhaps an hour or so later, the sound of the starter on the outboard motor woke me again, Laurie pulling on the cord as the engine sputtered a few times before catching. He lifted his fisherman pants around his thighs and sat down on the sidewall of the dinghy.

'Morning Laurie,' I said, rubbing my eyes. 'Where you off to?'

'Morning Jules. It's my seventieth birthday today,' he answered, soft but happy. 'I never thought I'd make it this far.'

'Happy birthday.' I smiled back. 'You going out for some time alone?'

Laurie shook his head, patted the pouch he sometimes kept around his middle when going ashore, and pointed to a large part-forested rock that stuck bolt upright from the sea.

'I think there's some telephone signal the other side of that small island there. I'm going to call my ex-wife.' He grinned boyishly. 'She knows the date. It'll ruin her day to know I'm still alive.'

Laurie twisted the throttle and put revs through the motor, then flicked it from neutral to drive with a crack of gears engaging. He gave me a nod and his regular thumbs-up as a small puff of smoke released from the engine and the dinghy peeled away from *Atlanta*'s side. His hair blew hard against his head as he raced away, the burgundy canvas of the dinghy bouncing high over the small waves.

The sun lifted, brightened, rising across the next hours while we experienced the now-familiar confusion at why Reinard was yet to announce any plans for the new day. Together with Jake and Laurie, I ate slices of papaya and melon, leaning on the coach house and watching flies kiss their trumpet at sugary juices upon the blade of a knife. The fruit was laid out on its shining steel platter, and three cups of tea orbited it as we ate noisily, throwing strips of rind overboard, where small fish appeared and began to feed. Nim reclined beside us, one hand trailing along the deck as her arm lounged from out of the criss-crossing green ropes of the hammock.

'Slow-moving depression coming up from the south.'

Laurie leaned forward, smiling at his own joke as Erik padded slowly down the deck, idling our way and rubbing his head. He took another piece of fruit as Erik came up, looking newly out of bed. Laurie pushed the platter towards him and spoke warmly, as if trying to mend any injury done by his impatience the previous night.

'Morning, Erik. Get some tucker inside you.'

Erik gave the simple smile that his face often wore, his nature always so easy-going and relaxed. With a paw-like hand, he grabbed two slices of fruit, the melon and papaya pinned together and lifted from the eager circle of our arms going in and out. We all ate, fruit crunching loudly in the silence.

'Anyone seen Reinard?' Jake asked.

Three heads went from side to side, as the crunching continued.

'I think he shaving,' Nim said.

'You'd think the guy would have come up with some sort of plan for filming before sailing all the way out here.' Laurie sounded perplexed at the thought of a job done badly. He pointed down to the dinghy beside the boat. 'Did you check the tank on the outboard, Erik? I think it might have been running low on fuel.'

Erik answered through a mouthful of melon, then gave a guilty giggle. 'I thought about it.'

Laurie shook his head to himself, spoke sternly. 'In marine terms, you don't *think* about checking anything. If you think about it then you do it. That's your subconscious talking to you. You know how to siphon fuel into the tank?'

'Yeah, yeah. I know.'

Erik went on eating, but didn't look up, and in the growing morning heat there was an impatience, as inescapable as the limits of the deck, and kept company by a sense of old tensions, resurfacing in the unorganised schedule where Reinard's masterplan was supposed to have been. The boat was gradually starting to seem more like a floating madhouse, or at least a nursery, so that whoever it was who irritated you, there were only so many steps you could take away from them before *Atlanta*'s deck came to an end. There was nowhere to go for a walk, and nothing on all sides but sea. Nearing midday-heat the problem always felt worse, with the rooms below deck oppressively hot, and the shade above limited to only a few small spaces. Sometimes I'd move to a pocket of shade further down the boat, only for *Atlanta* to turn slightly on her anchor and return me to the glaring heat of intense sunlight. Covering my skin and squinting in the brightness, I would look back down the deck to see the rest of the crew sitting in the inviting shelter of the shade, which a moment later I would remember was the only reason I had been so close to them to begin with. Either you endured the hot reddening of your skin, agitated further by the rubber or linseed oil that proofed and protected different parts of *Atlanta*'s anatomy, or you faced the company of your colleagues. When my skin told me it had had enough of heat, when the sweat trickled into my eyes, I would return to the fate of conversation and pace back down the deck into the shade.

An hour later there was no change but for the temperature, climbing hotter by degrees. Reinard had appeared from below deck and was milling around near the coach house, with still no word on the day ahead. Jake set down his pack of equipment, beside which the rope ladder led down to the dinghy. His fragile periscope of mirrors was placed carefully beside it, ready to fulfil his wish that those we interviewed be able to see his face when filming. I sat towards the bow, where Erik had disconnected the fuel line and lifted the tank out from the dinghy. He stood, his bare belly casting some of the best shade to be found, and his feet spread either side of the tank. On a raised section of the deck waited one of the larger cans in which petrol was stored, and in his hands he held the thin, clear tube that would siphon the fuel into the tank.

'It's pretty easy really.' Erik fondled the tube in front of him. 'You just keep the thing that you're moving fuel to at a lower level, and you suck on the tube without getting it in your mouth. But you have to be careful the fumes don't take your breath away, so that you suck it up by mistake.'

I nodded, eyebrows up, a little concerned at the way Erik was talking me through the stages of siphoning petrol and not just getting on with the job. I watched him, curiously lifting both ends of the tube in his hands. He shrugged as if in resignation, bound by the law of saving face to at least attempt it. Erik stuck one end of the tube in the petrol can, up on the raised portion of the deck. He leant over, feet either side of the tank he was refilling, the tube slipping through his goatee beard and between his thin lips. He sucked, though only a little, his eyes looking sidewards suspiciously, as if in anticipation of foul play from the laws of physics. Together we watched the fuel appear in the clear tube before hesitating at its apex, succumbing to gravity, and falling back down to the tank. Erik reset himself, shuffling his feet like a golfer, and with his lips drawn tight around the tube he sucked sharply. The petrol rose hard out of the can, shooting up to the high arc of the tube and then plummeting down fast, directly into his lips.

Erik roared. His cheeks filled and his chest heaved with coughing and retching and pain. He spat, petrol sprayed in a wide panorama as he turned red, eyes gaping black and horrified. He stumbled backwards, retching vapour and roaring some more. The commotion and the noise of that large man so wrongfooted alerted everyone down the deck, heads turned and Reinard's innocent voice rang out.

'What's wrong? Erik? Are you OK?'

Erik fell against the rail, his arms spread and shoulders heaving for new breath, saliva hanging from his lips as he spat repeatedly to clear the petrol from his mouth. Laurie stormed by Reinard, marched up to where we stood, shouted.

'No, he's not fucking OK, the idiot's swallowed gasoline.'

Laurie reached quickly for a small bottle containing a fire retardant, he pressed down at the industrial, childproof lid and turned it with a cracking as he moved to the bow and Erik reared up like some enraged grizzly bear who'd been shot but not killed.

'Get him – the hell – away – from me!'

Erik roared, roared dangerous, a finger large and direct at Laurie's face; the Alabaman towering twice the height and girth of the seventy-year-old man standing there, skinny in his fisherman's pants with his scrawny arms sticking from a baggy T-shirt. Laurie ducked by him with the fire retardant, a lime green gel that he squirted down and spread with a cloth where the petrol soaked into the dry wood of *Atlanta*'s deck. Erik hit a shade of crimson that faded to red, his eyes dropped halfway out his head, a chest heaving on fury and the man breathing rage and petrol deep from the lungs. Still reeling, he stumbled backwards with another fall, producing a sound of metal breaking underfoot as he crashed into Jake's waiting bag of equipment. I saw Jake leap up from further down the boat; he bit his lip in quiet panic and showed a pain no less palpable than the one still washing over Erik's face. Right away I knew what had happened, and no doubt about it: his periscope was broken. With scurrying steps, his pale skin jumped out from where he kept safe distance, sweeping the mangled knot of metal up in his arms and disappearing with it below deck.

All too late, Reinard discovered the instinct of a peacemaker. He raised his arms, palms down and his voice soft, gentle, calm.

'OK. OK. You're my crew. We won't have any violence here.'

Laurie ignored them both, busily fireproofing the deck. Erik went on breathing deep, with Reinard never about to appreciate that being simultaneously in charge and not at all in charge, setting a mood where nobody really knew what was going on, was a part of what built the volatility of the mood that week on board *Atlanta*.

It was emotional, watching Erik looking out at Surin. Silently he regained his breath and wiped the hairy back of his hand across his mouth. You could tell that Erik knew, perhaps not even so very deep down, that he possessed an elemental lack of competence. In him was an eternal childhood, a gentle nature and the softest insecurity. You saw it most of all in the moments when he made a joke and, immediately afterwards, looked hopefully at the faces of those around him to see their reaction, to check whether he'd done all right. I don't think he understood quite how much people naturally and genuinely liked him. Laurie would later tell me that it pained him the way they fought, but that sometimes his inabilities, not for want of trying, had proven dangerous on a boat. Other owners had figured out not to trust him with their ships, but Laurie charged himself as having been too soft in their time together; hadn't had heart to say it straight that Erik hindered more than he helped. The tendency was a dangerous one, and Erik's stubborn refusal to neither learn nor give up trying, you suspected, still had a way to run, and more problems to engender.

Words or Pictures – midday

Jake looked round, his head following the creak of the wooden step as I descended the ladder and eased down into the small room below deck. Normally so robotic in his manner, his face had turned sad, vulnerable; as if the bent box of metal and the broken shard of glass were his own insides being twisted. He tapped a small screwdriver on the bench beside the wreckage.

'Is it OK?' I asked.

He shook his head, eyes almost welling up. 'It can be repaired, but not here. We won't be able to use it for the documentary.'

I put a hand on his shoulder, and side by side we looked down at the curious piece of engineering, recently so exact and functional and now altogether useless.

'At least your cameras are all OK.'

He nodded and we stood in silence, Jake taking a deep breath of the warm air below deck, composing himself a little. *Atlanta* creaked, the mattress gave a sigh as he collapsed into it and sat down. The question had intrigued me for the last few days, and as he looked round with a resigned, weary smile, I decided to ask it then.

'What made you get involved in film to start with?'

He looked over, put down the screwdriver and gave, I thought, a quick gulp. He removed his thick-rimmed spectacles, beads of sweat running down his temples, burnt red from the minutes in the sun it took him to rub on cream. It befit his nature that he knew the reason right off. With Jake there was always precise explanation; no meandering thought pattern but a single, clear motive.

'It wasn't always the plan. I grew up pretty much on the doorstep of the Heathrow flight path. My father was a pilot all his working life, British Airways. He was from Glasgow, Govan. Working-class

Scottish family, poor, and he worked hard to get to where he is now, and to be comfortable. A large house near London, a chalet in the Alps. All that stuff. After university I was all set to follow him. I was going to be a pilot, because I quite liked planes. And I remember one day, when I was booked in to take the aptitude test for flying, we had a conversation about the job. And, I still remember what he said to me: "It's a good job. Travel, good pay. You won't change the world, but it's a good job."'

Jake gave a quiet laugh, 'And I thought, "What if I do want to change the world?"'

He paused a moment, not normally one for emotion but the stuff rising in him, seeming to help him recover composure in the nadir of his mood.

'My dad worked hard so that he could get out of poverty. And he did that so that I don't have to. I guess I thought it was a pretty stupid way to use that privilege, if I didn't try and do something more with it, not just carry on and repeat what he did.'

Jake looked at me a moment longer, such feeling in his cool eyes and his face at once kind but determined. A brief smile passed his lips, before he turned away and picked up his screwdriver again, lowering his head back to those lengths of twisted metal. He spoke into the desk, his face reflecting up from the piece of mirror.

'So I decided to study film and photography.'

'Is it working out?'

'I'm happy I'm not a pilot.'

'And you think images are what change people's minds about the world?'

Jake wasn't claiming that, he was too smart to believe anything in absolute terms, aside from the vague need that some sort of change was necessary. He shrugged, adjusted his glasses.

'I think they help, but they're not enough on their own. I feel quite jealous that you can just … you know, write, without all this.'

He paused, gestured to the bunk above: covered in hard drives, lenses, cases, cables and leads, two computers, small batteries, larger lithium batteries, cameras and the tripods and frames on which to mount them. He had a point.

'I get that, but I think people respect images more than words. It's a more valuable currency. People pay more for them, and people are more interested in them. So they are what will make change, because images are what people see, and where people's attention falls.'

Jake put the screwdriver back down. The sound of voices trying to reconcile differences came down the steps from above.

'They're looking at them, yes. But I'm not sure "attention" is what's happening. And anyway, if you believe that, then why do you write?'

I smiled at that old question. I still liked it, even if my answer had probably shifted over the years.

'Because I always did, and I guess I did it enough that I got to be OK at it.'

'But you don't believe books change things?'

'I used to.'

That was the honest truth, and it was a sadness, a defeat, to hear the thought expressed for the first time in my own voice.

'I used to believe they could change the world because they had changed my world. They'd made me believe in things that otherwise I wouldn't have, emotions I wouldn't have experienced. And those emotions shaped my life and how I led it.'

'You don't think that still happens?'

'Perhaps. I don't know.'

We sat next to one another on the bed, arms at our sides and hands rested on the edge of the bunk. The screws and rods and pieces of glass lay in the tiny chaos on the bench. Jake inhaled.

'Do you think it's different now? Do you think books were once important and now they're not?'

'Maybe. I think they still have the power to change a person's life in a way images can't. Because the reader is active in taking in and building the story, where the viewer of an image is passive, and doesn't have to create the vision in their own head. But I think it's changed. All the books I first fell in love with were from the nineteenth century, and humans were different then. I think we'd learned less and so we were able to believe in more, and books could capture all that was in our imagination better than anything else. It was OK to write about the human spirit, the meaning of being alive, the ecstasy of the world.'

'You don't think it's OK to do that any more?'

I considered it a moment. It did seem a grand declaration to make, so simplistic and naïve beside the wires and screens and devices in hard metal casing. Perhaps in stating it, and then recoiling awkwardly a little at my own words, I had proved my point.

'I think we're more reserved as a society, and as people, and books and media are meant to reflect that. But before' – I waited for the thought I felt forming to catch up with me – 'books were the foremost entertainment. They were graphic and scandalous and now they aren't. In the marketplace for entertainment, for lots of people, books are now only the first choice for people who want to be considered, calm, civilised, informed. I know it's not always like that, there are exceptions, but I don't think readers want to read anything that has too much feeling, or is angry, or that demands the world needs to change. That isn't the same mood people are in when they're sitting down with a book.'

Jake looked on, either thoughtful or distant, so that either I'd moved him or lost him altogether. He turned to me with a rare smile, a rarer moment of humour from that mind so technical. The smile broke into a kind laugh.

'Yeah, I guess they want something a bit more easy-going. Something that goes with coffee and cake.'

Don't Look at the Camera – afternoon

Erik was smiling again as the dinghy motored towards shore; still rubbing at his chest and his lips making the sickly expressions of a bad taste, but happy to be away from *Atlanta* and the site of his ignominy. Nim was with us in the boat, dressed proud and smart for the responsibility of her role as translator. A navy silk blouse was filling with the wind, and one hand held on to the wide cream-coloured brim of a hat covering her dark hair. With the back of her other hand she hit playfully at Erik.

'You not supposed to drink the fuel, Erik!'

She laughed hard in his face as Erik replied with a smile. I turned to Reinard, who was crouching beside Jake, playing with the zoom of one of the smaller cameras, moving it in and out of focus on a puddle of water between his sandals.

'What took you so long this morning, below deck?'

He looked round at me, bright blue eyes shining.

'I was having a shave.'

'But you were down there for over an hour.'

'I had some thoughts while I was shaving.'

'For over an hour!?'

'They were good thoughts.'

The boat continued over the tops of the waves, *Atlanta* with its maroon covers and white hull getting smaller behind us. The beachfront huts of Surin drew closer, just behind the lines of Moken *kabang*, tethered on lengths of rope and leaning to one side in the pale mud where the tide had retreated for the afternoon.

Back on Surin, Moo Hning, having agreed the previous day to be interviewed about Moken tradition, was away when we returned to her family's hut. When we arrived a young boy ran to fetch her, and as Jake unpacked a bag I walked along the row of modest houses, beneath their stilts and out towards the rocks and trees at the end of the village where beach met undergrowth. As my footsteps disturbed the quiet, a hen, followed by a line of three chicks, each maybe the size of a tiny yellow apple, fell down the slope of a steep bank, so that loose soil tumbled down and the large bird leapt quickly airborne. Its wings spread, then pushed backwards behind it, as feathers caught drag from the air and slowed the bird's fall, bringing it gracefully back to earth. One by one, the chicks edged forwards to the lowest portion of rock, then jumped down to their mother before the family shuffled forward in a line along the beach.

On a rock beneath the shadow of the forest, I sat down to wait for Moo Hning's return. Beside me was a squat fruit tree, weighed down by thin branches, which had dropped their windfall into a jam of yellows and reds about the base of the tree. Flocks of small birds flew from the undergrowth, hopping among the collapsing, bubbling fruit, where eager beaks pecked a meal from the remains. Upturned on the hard shell of its back lay a cockroach, dead and with spindly legs upright in the air, while a line of ants made their way past it in perfectly spaced formation; some holding small pieces of food or debris in front of them, the objects carried in pincers too small to see. Like iron filings repelled by a magnet, they each gave precisely uniform space to the ant ahead and behind, and so too the carapace of the cockroach they moved past. A little closer to the sea, large flies walked over the sand and gravel of the beach, wings translucent, folded out behind them as if a pair of parachutes that caught the light of the sun. Skipjacks with their fat fins pulled themselves between pools of water, stuck in an evolution half between land and sea, and clams crackled so that the empty flats of the beach popped like toasting corn in a pan.

On the upright of a nearby hut, a gecko waited, the suckers of its feet stuck faithfully to the bamboo so that the creature pointed back down towards the earth, while a line of ants made their way respectfully around the perimeter of its spread limbs and tail. A small lizard, dark green but with yellow splashed down one side, scurried over a rock and on to the earth, pulling a grub from the soil and jerking it backwards into its throat. The point of its jaw fastened shut, and then the hard line of its head seemed to my human eyes, and for just a single moment, to hold the slightest grin along its tiny, razor-edged teeth. The lizard's needle-like tongue was put away, and it climbed back to its rock, rubbing the side of its head against the surface, so that the scales of its skin sang softly with a sound of abrasion, and the opaque black ball of its eye moved close over the stone. In rapid shots of staccato movement it crawled back towards the forest, its body moving now so fast and next so still, one limb at a time, as it switched from animated back to frozen. As it went, the lizard passed a wet patch of beach, where on the surface of a small pool was a large ant, its wings seeming to pin it lucklessly against the water. The head of the lizard snapped fast towards it, mouth open as the ant disappeared. The lizard waited, motionless beside the rock, its meal altogether vanished save for a small droplet of water that glistened on its neck.

So long and so closely I watched it all, contextualising and considering their moves on my terms. The animals did not really wait, for waiting required time, and also a purpose being awaited, and both were constructs of which they must have been unaware. Eventually, my mind wandering, I grew almost uncomfortable with my voyeurism; unnerved as if some other creature were maybe observing *me* with similar intent. Perhaps a snake was keeping a watching brief on my position, maybe an eagle high overhead. Or was my brain really it: the upwards extremity in examination of life on earth? Consciousness and thought felt somehow sinister, almost as if it was an ulterior motive in that place of mere existence and survival. Could it have been that in all that jungle, of life so vast and so diverse, ours was the limit of thought, with humans the end-point of all the earth's consciousness? And if indeed that were so, how could we ever be equal to such a responsibility?

Often during that week, whether with the Moken, in the jungle or even with Laurie, I would find myself with the words of William Blake. His verse always crept back to my head, the 'Introduction' poem at the start of *Songs of Innocence*, where Blake wrote of a piper who 'stain'd the water clear' by singing a song about the joyous, unspoilt world he had found. Whatever I wrote, recorded, photographed, I always considered whether Blake's emphasis in that line was on the 'stain' or on the 'clear'. Was the human act of recording existence a thing that stained clarity, tainted but true, on to the random world we had found ourselves in? Or was it the opposite; were our efforts at recordings only ever to be a stain, tarnishing creatures and moments that had once been clear and pure, before we came along with our urge to document?

It was there, on the edge of a remote village which felt like the borders of the human world, that you saw the rest of human life on earth exposed for what it was. The Moken, in Reinard's view, were to be the focus that drew all else into relief and reminded us who we were supposed to be. They were essential, they were good; and in return for that glorious role in our imaginations they were to be afforded no complexity or detail that allowed them the luxury of human failing, vice or ambition away from this ancestral homeland.

Once Moo Hning had been fetched back by the young boy, she agreed once again to talk about Moken tradition and history, so that Reinard clapped his hands together in excitement.

'OK, so, perhaps here then?' he said, pointing to a rock beside the hut.

'It doesn't look very comfortable for her,' replied Jake, 'and it's probably a bit dark here. Nim, could you ask if there's somewhere else? Somewhere that's not too dark, not too bright and, preferably, in front of a house, to give a feeling of tradition.'

Nim asked Moo Hning in Thai if there was another place we could sit. Somewhere that was not too dark, nor too bright and, preferably, in front of a house, to give a feeling of tradition. Moo Hning nodded, and together we all walked through the lines of huts, two-deep, that comprised the village. Moo Hning went arm-in-arm with Nim, while Erik and Reinard followed behind with microphones and a second camera. Jake had a point in his earlier remarks, and never before had writing seemed to me so dignified, respectful, courteous and discreet; to take only a pen and a notepad instead of the caravan of equipment and ulterior motive with which we traipsed through someone else's community. The bamboo houses were each fronted by a porch: a small platform where families cooked and ate. After a few minutes of slow, encumbered walking, Jake came to a halt and held up his light metre. He muttered the number to himself, then cast his arm over the location.

'Here's good. We can sit her inside the porch, and use the structure of the hut to give a frame within a frame. That will make it look nicer.'

Speaking delicately, Nim encouraged a perplexed Moo Hning into the porch of the house. Jake set down his tripod, mounting the camera and inspecting the contents of the frame. Moo Hning shuffled awkwardly as Erik switched his role from captain's mate to sound engineer and clipped a small microphone to the collar of her blue blouse, letting the wire fall behind to a recorder with a thin antenna. With his large palms proffered in reassurance, he backed away and extended the telescopic pole that held his boom microphone, shielded from any wind or stray noise by its full, fluffy plumage. Above the short ledge was a thin washing line with towels on one side, so that Jake repositioned a purple towel that was drying there, and pulled it into the frame; providing detail of colour to the otherwise dark, uneventful background against which Moo Hning sat. Beside her was a stack of cooking pots, set upon a low shelf that stood on splintering tiptoes, where either ants or termites had eaten through most of its once-square legs, leaving small coronas of wood dust around the narrow point of each foot.

Levelling his tripod in the sand, Jake moved the camera back a short distance, so that within the camera's view there appeared the frame of the porch outside the hut. Jake aligned the right angles of each precisely. The purple towel offered a sense of visual depth, so that the eye understood more clearly the distance between Moo Hning and her setting. Carefully, Jake composed and made perfect sense of that scene, so that other brains would never have to trouble to explain the pixels with which they were presented. Moo Hning sat in the context of a frame for which nobody needed turn their head, a depth understood without any movement in the muscle of a retina focused for hours on end on a television screen. With a domestic context perfectly suited to explain the words about tradition that would follow, no effort was spared that might help to set that emperor of a viewer, in the throne of their armchair or settee, entirely at ease.

I stooped down beside Jake, eye-height with both Moo Hning and the lens. Just out of frame, Erik stood opposite, holding the boom microphone over her head.

'Up a little,' said Jake, raising a hand as I watched the fluffy shape rise up on the small monitor beside me.

'How's that?'

'Little bit more.'

The four fingers of Jake's upturned palm flicked a little, and then a little more, and then the shape ascended out of view. Through the patient translation of Nim, it was explained to Moo Hning that I would ask questions and Nim would translate them into Thai. Moo Hning would answer, but in Moken, looking towards me and Nim rather than the camera. With a nod of understanding, an air of nervousness and the final call of 'Rolling!', we began. Even in a foreign language, you could still hear in her voice that Nim was enjoying taking up the soft tones of a television presenter greeting an interviewee, as she translated a first question into Thai.

'What is the history of the Moken?'

Moo Hning gave a little smile and turned to look straight down the black glass barrel of the lens, before starting to deliver her answer.

'Cut!' said Jake. 'She's looking straight at the camera, Nim, that means she's looking straight at the audience. Can you ask her to look at you and pretend the camera's not there?'

Jake mimed it, covering the lens with a hand. Nim translated, Moo Hning smiled again. She nodded, and repositioned herself.

'OK. She understand,' said Nim.

'Rolling!' rang out again, and with silent coaxing from myself and Nim, Moo Hning began to talk once more, looking diligently at Nim and speaking in a familiar tone that Nim nodded along to in what looked like total understanding.

Jake and I turned to one another as he mouthed the words. 'Is she speaking Thai?'

'Cut!' It came again, Moo Hning a little startled, sure that she had done as she had been asked and wasn't looking at the camera.

'Nim, was that Thai?' Jake asked.

Nim turned, nodded.

'Can you ask her to speak Moken, please?'

Nim turned to Moo Hning, spoke Thai with a strong emphasis on the one word in the sentence that Jake and I were hoping to hear: *Moken*. Moo Hning looked perplexed. Hesitantly she spoke to Nim in Thai, as if not wanting to talk out of turn, reluctant to doubt the intentions or intelligence of people carrying so many black boxes of glass and metal; things that captured perfect images, that took time and technical adjustments to assemble and were so heavy they must have been expensive. Nim looked round at us.

'She say, "But none of you understand Moken."'

Erik rolled his eyes a little, as if Moo Hning was the stupid one.

I followed up. 'We know, but it's not for us, it's for the audience.' I pointed to the camera. 'And it's a programme about the Moken, about Moken culture. We'll translate it later and the words will be on the screen in English.'

Nim repeated the instruction. Moo Hning's brow creased as she answered.

Nim turned back to us. 'She say you say to pretend camera not there.'

Jake and I looked at one another, wrapped up in the unwritten rules and white lies of an anthropology documentary, all of us stitched up in an absurd bind between authenticity and common sense. She had a point. Moo Hning let out a sigh, spoke more. Nim turned to us.

'She say why you change language to Moken, to Thai, and then to English. She say it no make sense. Easier speak Thai.'

And Nim gave a frustrated shake of her head, accentuated by the flapping brim of her flat. In all regards, save for capturing the authenticity of an indigenous culture, thrilling for its remoteness and integrity, Moo Hning was entirely correct.

'We know,' appeased Jake. 'But if you can just ask her to forget about that, look at you, and talk Moken. That would be perfect.'

Nim relayed the instruction, to which Moo Hning laughed uncertainly, but with another call of 'Rolling!' and Moo Hning looking dutifully into my eyes, she began to speak in the lower and slow, sonorous tones of the Moken language. Rhythmically the words came to us: calm, peaceful and utterly without meaning in our ears. Occasionally she stuttered, or paused between one word we did not understand and the next word we did not understand, so that we all waited with a peculiar hope that the camera's microphone was filling with the words we wanted and expected. We listened, clueless as to what Moo Hning was saying, but the tones of her language so fluid, gentle and regular like the waves, that it seemed a perfect fit with the stories in which she had grown up and now passed on. Three years later, with Reinard still unable to find a translator for his project, I wrote up the rudimentary version that Nim had provided us, after asking Moo Hning to repeat what she had said in Thai.

'The history of the Moken people is a long, long history. We struggle always to survive, life always very hard. The history goes back hundreds and hundreds of years, and the story begins with the ancient island princess, Sibian. Her husband was unfaithful with her sister and so the Moken people were cast out and lost to the sea. In our language, *Mo* means sinking and *ken* means water ... so we were a people cursed always to be drowned, and now we move always between islands, because the sea is our home. All through our history it has been this way. When we move between islands, always by boat, and always just to survive, we tell the stories from our ancestors: teaching us about the sea, and about our boats.'

Just as their existences were described always in terms of 'surviving' and never 'living', so too were families always referred to as 'ancestors', even those from only a generation or two before, relatives who would have been regarded as great-grandparents in Western culture. The stories were imbued with spirituality, romance and a leaning towards mysticism that made our English so ruthless and precisely scientific in comparison. William Burroughs had regarded language as a virus, grammar a thing still worse: a codified form of thought that cannibalises the mind, murdering with it the impulse of ideas taking shape without need of structure.

Some five minutes later, with none of us able to understand a word Moo Hning had said, she was still going. Jake and I looked at one another, Erik's arms sagged with the weight of the boom pole. Jake tapped Nim on the shoulder and mouthed, 'Is she nearly finished?'

Nim interrupted in a loud, impatient call of Thai. Moo Hning was shocked, sure she'd been doing it right. She replied with a shake of the head, a perturbed expression that showed quite clearly she thought us hasty. The idea of condensing centuries of oral history into forty-second audio clips was clearly quite alien to her. With a puzzled expression she answered Nim in Thai, and Nim translated without turning, 'This just beginning.'

Slightly puzzled, Moo Hning resumed, her voice coming across a little distant, as if she were proceeding through our other questions, but no longer sure if we really did or did not want to know her stories. Moo Hning was not one to edit or abridge for the sake of brevity in a final programme she could not conceive of. All her stories had been told on calm beaches, with other ready listeners, each with their own stories to share, and no impatience for the conceit of a digestible version. On occasions when Nim translated for us from Thai, one sentence at a time, it felt as though in each new sentence Moo Hning would re-clarify a point from the previous sentence, so building an overlapping picture of her tale that was gradually made plain.

Above my head, as Moo Hning went on speaking in Moken, I watched a mosquito appear and fly towards a porch, as if wondering whether it was safe inside the home. On the diagonally cut threshold between light and shade it hovered in the air, causing a spider to scuttle tentatively out of a crevice and down the verticals of its web, in readiness for the next move of the other creature. Outside a few chickens, a duck and a rooster waddled out from behind a nearby cabin to look at us curiously. The duck cocked its head, the broad yellow bill sticking out our way. Its eyes settled on us, quite suspicious at this gathering of humans and lenses in the path where its webbed feet normally plodded unimpeded down the beach.

Indigenous Code – afternoon

Erik, Reinard and Jake roamed free with cameras while I walked through the village, those two hundred metres of Surin that contained all human activity between ocean and dense jungle. During the daytime, when the men were away fishing or shepherding tourists, the Moken women had the run of the beachfront. There they wrote line after line of code, spinning an indigenous internet in the shade beneath their stilt huts. *Gasbagging* was what Laurie had called it, his name for the gossiping and speculating by which they told stories both true and tall, for Moo Hning to then repeat in the shade of another hut back at Rawai. Although she had never been there before, her family on Surin knew exactly who she was, just as she knew them, and all by virtue of stories relayed by mouth and even many months apart. Through such exchanges they would know what all their families were doing, deep into their spoken futures.

The folklore was made possible by empty time, and the Moken, for all their economic poverty and adversity, and despite the occasional tourist to tend to, were at least their own boss. Capital was bound by geography, and while it moved in borderless flows, its concerns in the region gravitated to hubs in Singapore, Kuala Lumpur and Bangkok, so that whatever happened on Surin was largely worthless to it. Inside every hut waited a complete absence of anywhere to spend money; the waves mocked gently at the presumed usefulness of those rectangular pieces of paper that bore the image of a monarch in my pocket, and laughed harder at the plastic card bearing random numbers in my luggage. Back on *Atlanta*, Laurie would laugh when I mentioned the oddity of having nowhere to spend any money, even if you wanted to. 'You want to try going into Polynesia, Vanuatu and out that way. They've got no money and the only currency is pigs.

Hit one of those pigs when you're driving and you wipe out a guy's life savings; there's hell to pay.'

From Surin, the wealth of the world appeared as a tripartite of monetary capital, time, and space, with few people ever permitted more than two of the three. Admittedly there were extreme outliers of the rule and, in all they took for themselves, those aboard the super yacht – owned by a New World Order or otherwise – distorted the comfort and economic claims of everyone below them. The Moken, like those who I had once met on the Kazakh steppe, had all the time and space they could wish for, but had to endure financial precarity as gaping as the landscape they could call their own. Those I knew back in London had money but not enough of it to afford either free time or a great deal of space in the cramped, expensive financial hub that sustained them. Sometimes the very wealthy might have been permitted both money and space, but had to devote so much of their life to maintaining that level of income that they too fell at the hurdle of having time to savour wealth a little more enjoyably. The Moken, with all of their space and their time, enjoyed an endless supply of the spare days and hours required to uphold the oral tradition that chronicled, among other things, life's struggles on the very edge of an economic world. It wasn't poverty that they were living, for poverty would have also required the presence of riches, which were nowhere to be seen. At the same time, I did not feel comfortable romanticising their existence, for though few seemed unhappy, there was no denying that more basics of food, shelter, electricity and medicine would have done something to improve the quality of Moken life.

As a result of those great expanses of empty hours, all through Surin, whenever you asked how long away something was, the timing of it was always a mystery. 'Tomorrow' meant not the next day, but only the future, just as 'yesterday' meant nothing more precise than the past. They had no need of time, for nobody was going anywhere. Being in the right place at the moment of *Atlanta*'s departure back to Phuket, for both Moo Hning and Pho Nau, seemed like a vanishingly rare instance in which either woman had – with life-depending urgency for a fare they otherwise could not afford – given any thought to an actual appointment in a schedule. Even then, we farang had slipped far from rigid Western time to one that was more in keeping with boats, tides and islands. There was morning, after-noon, evening. Occasionally the detail was finessed into first or last thing, but that was all.

As I wandered along the beach, wiling my own time, a woman sat smoking a rolled cigarette in the shadows beneath one of the huts. She turned as she heard me walk by; large bare breasts hung at her middle with a baby attached at one of them. The baby's mouth was docked upon her nipple, which spread wide and purple-brown across an area most of the size of its head. She caught my eye, all smiles where red-stained betel shone in the sunlight. On her cheeks were the dull, crimson pits and pocks of a fading acne, and in her hand the rough paper of the palm leaf cigarette, rolled and cradled, slow-smouldering between her fingers. Black curls of hair blew on the sea wind, and she looked to be an age rare on that island; for she was young, at least a little while longer. On Surin nearly everyone looked like children or old people, as if life aged them fast once they passed whatever rites of passage admitted them to adulthood and brought an end to the allowances of being a child. Either that, or those of working age had simply left as soon as their years allowed it.

Nearby I heard those who were still children as they went about a constant play. One mother pulled back her son by his arm, rubbed white mud across his cheeks and forehead, so that he took on the same ghostlike pallor of the other young faces protected against that tropical sunlight. He ran screaming from her, joining friends as the group chased one another down the beachfront. They pulled at the tails of cats, pursued the geese and chickens beneath the floors of the stilt huts. Stout little legs pounded plumes of sand up behind them, and then came the crack, the explosive thud, echoing, as a boy's legs kept on running right past the point at which his head hit the underside of a hut: he connected full against low bamboo timbers, and with a loud bang his forehead struck the force of a full-blooded mallet blow. The boy hung a moment, all but horizontal in mid-air, and then landed with the sound of a thump in the glove of soft sand. His friends turned, pointing immediately with only loud laughter and no sympathy. The boy got up, rubbed his temples and shook the daze off of his head. He laughed back, laughed loud and from the throat; no thought of pain because there was no adult witness to mark any need for concern. Even had there been, it seemed unlikely much worry would have been forthcoming, for theirs was a childhood not like ours. The child got back to his feet, ran on, still laughing, screaming. Reinard had said early on that, at birth, a Moken child was submerged in pagan baptism into the waters of the Andaman. Those children were rough stones smoothed by the sea. Moken life was not a soft place, but that seemed not to concern them in the least, and they would never know anything different.

In one exception to the absence of commerce, beneath one of the huts, on a small, neat table, a young woman sold a modest collection of necklaces made from seashells, and T-shirts with an illustration of Surin printed on the front. A Japanese tourist with a camera over his shoulder nodded agreement at a price for two of the necklaces held between the woman's fingers. She handed them over, took a single note of currency in return, and then lifted up her fingers, looking at them in search of a price waiting at the end of a calculation of which she was unsure. Fingers lifted up and down, a moment of uncertainty settled. She looked at the note and its line of digits, at a box of notes and coins on her table, and then at her calculator with its ten possible digits and half dozen functions. She giggled, then laughed, and then handed the calculator uncertainly over to the tourist, motioning that he should enter the figure she needed. With a smile he did so, turning the screen and running his finger along it. He took the correct notes from the box, lifting them purposefully out and pointing to the digits to help communicate the transparency of his sums. I watched, reminded that even these digits – the curved or sharp forms of nine numbers and a zero, and so too the arithmetic which connected them like mathematical runes – were themselves only manufactured systems; ideas, philosophies and manmade constructs, designed to make commoditised life easier for a human brain. They bore no foundation in the natural world and there on Surin, as with time, numbers barely existed.

In the late afternoon, the temperature still uncomfortably high, we all regrouped, sitting down to eat at the hut of Moo Hning's family. On the island, everything was always too hot except for the food. Each meal was cooked on top of small ceramic blocks, filled with charcoal and the heat rising to the base of the pan through tiny squares set in a grid. The things were clay red, stained black at the bottom, and after they had been sufficiently well used and scorched, they cracked and were discarded, so that old shards lay scattered outside of each hut. Despite the tropical heat, the basic nature of the cooking fuel and equipment meant food had always turned unappealingly tepid by the time it was served, and had about it the vague sense of germs.

However far from ideal this was, there was no alternative. Electricity was a luxury, and it was only once night descended that a diesel generator came to life with a belch and then began to purr. For three hours it brought electricity, and so light, to those huts along the sands. Light being comparatively easy to generate by electricity, and heat intensive, there was no possibility of using the generator for cooking, and certainly the Moken would have been unable to afford the transport costs of bringing more fuel than was required for those hours of evening lighting. Picking through the lukewarm and crusty shells of small, scabby prawns and the stalks of tough, fibrous greens, you saw the luxury of modern shopping, and also why Moo Hning, Pho Nau and most others with an opportunity to pay their passage, had generally chosen – oblivious to the prejudices they would face there as nomads – to try their luck taking up on the mainland.

Whatever the germ of truth in, it wasn't entirely so cut and dry. The Moken who lived on Surin also professed without any doubt that they too had chosen the best of all possible lives for themselves, there in 'paradise' – the one word of English that most of them seemed to have learned. Those who had made a break for the mainland were no less convinced of the wisdom in their decision. As with people everywhere, the Moken had created different and universal truths to explain why their own choices, circumstances and ideas were the correct ones. Meanwhile, and with a thought of the pampered city I knew back home, I wondered if the role of the Moken on Surin was to act as custodians for a spirituality the rest of our world had long since left behind. We looked to them to provide us with a purity, a sense of the human that we still cherished, but no longer wanted for ourselves.

In early evening we readied a return to *Atlanta*, the sun coming down slow from our spot just above the equator. Cumulonimbus built up a vast mountain range along the horizon, cut with strokes of grey but a thin, brightly shining pink edge sketched along its topmost level. The last light poured in to cast shadows from the longtail boats left leaning in the mud, children running up and down the ropes that tethered them. Every human face was bathed in a warmth that shone back the tiredness of a day's end, and pools of water in people's discarded footprints picked out the sun in tiny golden crowns littered up and down the beach.

'We should get some of this,' said Jake.

He knelt down for 'magic hour', that time of day – at first but particularly last light – where the sun lights this earth to perfection and so all over the world, photographers drop to their knees in respect, and begin to unpack kit. I promise you, a disproportionate amount of world media, and especially that intended to evoke feeling, chronicles only what is going on at early evening of a bright day without too much cloud cover.

Jake mounted his camera into its Steadicam; a contraption of pivots and pistons that cradled the camera lovingly, isolating it so as to cushion the lens and image from the abrupt shocks of human footfall. With Steadicam in hand, Jake took short, patient steps down the beach, holding the rig out in front of him, its stabilisers and struts all sliding and adjusting to keep the camera balanced and perfectly level. Jake walked just behind the line of boats, catching their silhouettes as all of his chest, arm and shoulder muscles tensed with the effort of holding the camera in one position. After a few seconds, walking behind them, he turned his body; the gimbal of the rig obediently attuned to his movement, guiding the lens as it rotated out towards the sea and that glorious bank of cloud. The image in the monitor floated dreamily, so that the watching audience would one day glide down that beach as though they themselves were watching from a cloud, a horse-drawn carriage, magic carpet or in some other graceful, frictionless fashion befitting their celestial significance.

Laboon – evening

Laurie threw down the cleaver on the chicken's neck, slipped a paring knife in its asshole and up to its belly before pushing in his hand and pulling out the innards. He turned the bird on its front, put down the knife with a clatter of reflected light, picked up the cleaver again and struck it hard against the lower legs, detaching the feet and making a nearby glass of cutlery jump with a rattle. Beside him at the counter, I sliced through potatoes, opening up a few dusty burrows of black where larvae tumbled out and a maggot delved inwards, retreating from the blade before sliding down the helter-skelter of peel and on to the wooden grain of the chopping board. Small but plump, it wriggled there until I swept it away.

Further down deck, Nim stood over the hot plate, tending crescents of orange pumpkin in a proud line against the matt black grill. She sprinkled salt between finger and thumb, and slender slips of garlic browned at the edges, giving off a sweet aroma as gently they began to burn. I watched her remove the pith from the edge of the pumpkin seeds, dropping them into an envelope that next day she would give to Moo Hning's family as a gift to grow in the fertile soil of Surin, where the Moken, reliant on food aid of mainly rice from the government, seemed to produce little carbohydrates of their own. In a deep plastic bucket was a pile of washing-up from the previous evening, where flies kissed the blades of knives and prongs of forks, hovering at the streaks of oil and soy sauce that smeared down the faces of plates. On the far side of the deck the sun was disappearing, and all the cloud along the eastern horizon had turned to a deep and solid grey, although higher and to the west the sky remained a vibrant blue. The last of the sun glowed a rich shade of red, forcing a pocket through the grey cloud and then slipping a little way along it, like molten steel poured into the cold cast of a forge.

In the opening above the ladder, I could see Jake's pale head, still pink with sun, and I watched over his shoulder as the different images of the day loaded on to his computer. There was the sunset in one window, the talking head of Moo Hning, images of children playing and men fixing tangled knots in their fishing nets. A couple of the images had been frozen still, a couple more ran onwards, as history returned into the present through those moving frames; a short jump of time travel back to the afternoon, displayed in moving photocopies of a reality now past. Jake worked through the memory cards of his cameras, importing the data to his computer and then to an external hard drive. I watched those visions of the day's earlier life, playing simultaneously, and as I did I thought of the power implicit in the moving image. Dziga Vertov, don't doubt it, was the starting-point of modern history. The twenty-first century had actually begun in 1929 when *Man with a Movie Camera* became the first real attempt to showcase what humans were capable of with that new tool of motion picture held in our hands.

John Berger had tried to describe the shift, and he reasoned that traditional portrait and landscape paintings, from days when technological progress was confined to increasing precision in paint brush and paint colour, still shared a common feature with new images being recorded, even as the camera was invented and humans began to capture still photographs. Whatever the changes, both forms remained somehow in harmony with an old world in which people could still be simpler beings. The still image, however lifelike, would always be, in essence, a fake, because we knew the real world to be mobile, shifting. In addition to this limitation, drawings, paintings and photographs always made the spectator, standing in front of them, the assumed centre of the image. Berger reasoned that the creation of the film camera, by its movement, showed that there was no centre in the new world coming.

Still images, however they were recorded, had always been a time machine, an exteriority. They were a visual imprint of a moment that could by virtue of the image be retrieved at a later moment. It was an image of a past memory, a future or a fantasy, but made tangible and real in ways our mind could never internally create. To see a moment, recorded inside the single frame of a canvas or photograph, was a perception of a recognisable but nevertheless new likeness – a visual trinket to be consumed as easily as if it were candy for the imagination. With the movie camera, the stakes had been raised higher still; immersion was all but complete, so that people could see a series of continuous images, recorded from different perspectives, existing simultaneously with their own lives, and interacting harmoniously with one another. That was not only a new likeness but a new reality, one in which the counterfeit was harder to resist. From there on, humans had commanded the power to create and witness infinite new, living worlds; more worlds than any God or gods had ever managed, and so our meaning of who we were, and what part humans played in a life we had long struggled to understand, was destined to come tumbling down into sprawling, disorienting possibilities.

In that hot room below, Jake went on sorting images and data; the glowing screen of a computer now a receptacle for all the icons of files and folders that would once have been cardboard sleeves hung inside a cabinet. Something about the Moken, and something of the timelessness upon Surin, where almost everything was material and only the stories and memories abstract, showed our modern life in a peculiar light. We took the names of old, physical things to explain and lend meaning and order to the groupings of information that never left lines of digital code or two-dimensional life on the screen. The physical world of Surin, of wood, bamboo and water, held up a mirror to the series of noughts and ones that were programmed to activate a new motor or circuit when electricity flowed in them.

Watching Jake order the day away for some future edit, I thought more of Berger, considering whether he'd left his thought half-complete. As the camera showed Moken children running down the beach, the centre of the image was moving, but the spectator – sitting in their chair – was as central and unmoving as the assumed audience of any old, motionless portrait of an ambassador. In this way, a still image remained in keeping with belief in the existence of God, because although a painting or photo could capture an image that had otherwise expired, moved on in time, it was still only a single image from a single perspective. It was static, unchanging, monolithic and – just like God – a single truth. It did not shift to reveal new truths, and so was limited in the ability to make its own story, relying instead on whatever story the viewer imposed on it or the creator could hint at. That same single image, limited in the perspective it could show, shared the same basis as monotheism. As those images multiplied into moving images, containing scenes of life no different to the ones that immersed the viewer, so had we all fallen into a world of multiple simultaneous realities, a place in which the framed recordings looked no different to the unframed visions in our eyes. Thus did our certainty begin to collapse, until so many worlds overlapped, rivalling our own eyes, that we no longer knew which one to believe in. God was a single static image, or perhaps a single story; meanwhile humans had somehow learned to catch and trap the reality of multiple stories and multiple ages, from all angles. By sheer force of numbers, seeing such fantastic things – whether they were born of fiction or of truth – again and again, human minds had been liberated of their old limitations, freeing life itself to become ever more sedentary.

At one of the raised sections of the deck we sat together, gathered around plates with the pumpkin laid out next to a bowl of chicken and vegetable broth. In a large bowl was a mixture of rice and fried vegetables that also included some leftover oysters from the previous day. Nim passed the rice and oysters towards Reinard, who put up his hands to decline gratefully.

'No thank you, Nim. I don't eat the seafood here any more, at least not the cleaners.'

'Why not?' Jake asked, through a mouthful of rice.

'They're the bottom of the food chain, so they filter all that is in the sea, and there is so much pollution here now, so much mercury and nickel. When a battery on a boat is finished with, they are never disposed of properly, and so it all leaks back into the water. I'm sure it's OK to have a little, but not when you live here and would eat it all the time. It's a big problem for children.'

Reinard gave an embarrassed nod, apologetic at ruining anybody else's enjoyment of their meal. There was a silence, calm but for the waves and the sound of cutlery tapping on plastic plates. It had been a long day, and in true human fashion, nobody seemed particularly concerned at what the food would or would not do to them over the course of decades.

'We have no oysters when I was a child, no seafood.'

'Where did you live, Nim, before you moved to be with Laurie?'

'In north Thailand. Up in the hills, near Isaan. My family still live there, a long way from sea, on a farm. I do not miss it, but was a good place to grow up, very different. I help with many things there, all my life. We keep lots of animals, to eat and to sell, and when I was a child I had jobs like helping give birth to baby pigs, to pull them out when mama can't give birth herself.'

'You prefer life on the water, the islands?'

Nim nodded, chewing as she talked; oyster and rice and flakes of red chilli masticated against teeth. Jake set down his bowl, picking up a bottle of soy sauce and shaking its thick brown liquid so that it spread and stained the white of the rice.

'Life there is hard but good. I think it give me good heart. Now I can feel when people have good heart and when people have bad heart. I feel like Moken people here have good hearts.'

'Are your family still on the farm?' asked Jake.

'My mama still in Isaan, my father, he died one day when I was child. We all so sad that day.'

'I'm sorry.' Jake looked back down at his bowl as Nim gave a shrug.

'Lots of people in the hills die from fevers from mosquito. One day I came home and my father has fever. Malaria. I stayed with him in bed for two days. And after two days he died. When he died I remember I cry, and cry and cry. Life is always very difficult for people on farms here, but after he die it was more difficult.'

We went on eating in silence, a small bowl for the broth beside our plates, everyone taking their fingers to the small pieces of meat, gritting teeth and pulling their head away to part the old and rubbery flesh from the solid bone of a mature bird; a chicken that had long ago turned rooster, its flesh all muscle and sinew and the stuff so tough you had to swallow it in large morsels, defeated, when the fibres refused to break down any smaller. Laurie let out a curt laugh and muttered to himself, his mouth close to the next waiting bone, and as if talking to the meat itself.

'That's one old bird.' Jaw clenched, Laurie's head pulled from the bone, tearing at it with small drops of broth landing to shine on the table. Intermittently, he talked and chewed.

'It's a long time since that was a chicken. I get 'em from the local farmers, I like to support 'em, but that's not right for eating. Might be time to start going back to the supermarket, I reckon.'

A few polite chuckles rippled from lowered heads. Stubborn shreds of that old grey bird still seemed to be wedged between my teeth for the journey back to London almost a week later. It often felt like we got down to the business of eating with minimal pleasure at the taste involved. You had to work hard to savour the brief moment on the palate – some salt in the rice, the sweetness of the carrot between its watery stock, a general sense that you were providing sustenance to your body. It wasn't gourmet, but it was good enough and without pretence, meals as honest as they came.

Reinard was the first to finish, tipping his bowl to his mouth and drinking the last of its juice before resetting it on the deck. He sucked in his lips, his tongue poking out minutely to lick them clean as he coughed to clear his throat.

'Tomorrow, I would like us to see if we can interview Chief.'

That wasn't a bad statement; perhaps Reinard had a plan after all, the man just a slow starter, waiting to hit rhythm, and the schedule and intent for his documentary was about to get under way. Jake looked up from his food, Erik too, with an eagerness that betrayed its own insincerity, as if work were the thing that showed the limits of his abilities, but which he had to remain well-disposed towards. Everyone waited for Reinard to go on.

'The last time I was here was right after the tsunami, just after Christmas Day in 2004. I came once I heard the wave had struck, to deliver supplies of food, medicine and building materials. That was when I met Chief's father. He was a wise and noble man who had helped his people flee, before the tsunami destroyed everything.'

The wise and the noble part may have been true, it may have been myth. By then I didn't trust Reinard not to see whatever he wanted to where Moken wisdom was concerned. But still, it was nice to find purpose in him, something beyond only the idea of our aimlessly roaming back and forth with cameras.

'All across the Indian Ocean, communities were wiped out when the tsunami hit. But the Moken survived. For me, this is the finest example of the Moken wisdom, because the Moken had told for generations of the story of *laboon*.'

Reinard stared intently as he spoke the word, so that his eyes opened wide like the sound of its long Os. An enchantment settled on his face with the half glow of the deck light.

'The word translates into English as "the wave that consumes everything". And the story says that if the sea retreats very suddenly and far further from the shore than normal, it is a warning that a wave will then return the sea back to land with an almighty force.

So where seismologists and modern instruments failed to save more developed communities around Asia – places with much more technology – the Moken, with only their history of watching the sea for hundreds of years, and telling one another of its most remarkable and useful stories, survived. People here like to joke that the fish warned them.'

Reinard laughed softly at the simplicity of it. He was spellbound by his own storytelling but for once justified in his esteem, and so he went on explaining to us a story of events that had, for months and years on end, made the villagers of Surin the prized attraction of an international media circus. We were only the latest and the least prepared in a long line of film crews to show up on the island, each one more eager than the last to capture the story of a community that survived entirely unscathed from a natural disaster that by rights should have annihilated them. I shuddered to think of the schools, hospitals, sanitation, solar panels and battery storage that could've been installed on Surin with the millions of dollars of audio-visual hardware that must have been brought to document how these mystical wave-dodgers allegedly needed none of it.

'Before the tsunami hit,' Reinard went on, 'fishermen on boats in the Andaman all said they saw dolphins swimming further out to sea. The dolphins felt the earth beneath the water as it moved, and so they swam away from land. Villagers also reported that elephants in the forests in Sri Lanka went up to the hills. The way the Moken are in tune with their natural world is like magic. When the wave hit, and it hit with devastating impact, every stilt hut on that beachfront was shattered, but everyone in the village survived because the old chief led them inland and they made their way to higher ground in the jungle.'

'I heard one guy died,' Erik interjected inconveniently.

'Yes, I think there was one elderly man, he was disabled and couldn't move fast enough. But only one death, one death in two hundred people! People who lived in a village on a beach.'

That detail wasn't quite so flattering for the Moken, but it was nevertheless not one to trouble Reinard, who kept shaking his head in wonder. One way or another, perhaps Chief was to be it, the story that we'd been waiting for to give us our momentum.

Polynesian Narcotics – Saturday, midnight

Whether it was the anchor alarm, the heat, or moving above deck only to be caught by light rain blowing across *Atlanta*'s bows, I had no idea in the end how many days it was that I didn't sleep for more than two hours at a time. It became normal to find myself awake for a greater proportion of every twenty-four hours than I was used to, witnessing a broad spectrum of different nights and daylights in the sky over Surin.

'Insomnia' never seemed quite the right word for it. To me, insomnia had always been an inability to sleep that was perhaps in some ways irrational, unexplained. Aboard *Atlanta*, I generally knew exactly why it was I couldn't sleep, and there were always a host of other causes waiting once the most pressing had been resolved. Laurie would reassure me that this was nothing so unusual, and over his many years at sea he had got used to only ever sleeping for twenty minutes at a stretch, so accustomed had he become to checking on a course all through a long night.

An hour or so after midnight, drawn above deck again by the heat and the smell of papaya seeping back from the walls and rubber mattress, I saw that like the night before it, light shone from Laurie's small quarters on to the dim deck, crossed by the silhouetted right angles of rigging and cable. Laurie was looking out to sea, with a book set down next to him, and the shape of Surin dark like a huge whale breaking the surface of the night horizon. The sound of snoring came up from below, and looking down I saw Erik on his back, his belly rising and falling with loud snorts, his tattooed arm folded across his hairy chest. Reinard was beside him, on his side but with a whistle coming intermittently from his thin parted lips. Eyelids down, their faces turned so soft, content and innocent, some further evidence for the truth that everyone returns to childhood when they sleep. I cocked my thumb through the opening towards the pair, scratched my head and stifled a yawn.

'A boat is a pretty male place.'

'Sure is, Jules. If you're missing female company, just flash a smile at one of those island girls next time you're ashore.'

I laughed, embarrassed, but Laurie only nodded in his earnest way, absolute in his sincerity. My face straightened.

'Really?' I asked.

'Ahh, fuck yeah, Jules, they'll show you a good time, don't you worry about that.'

Laurie waved his hand my way, as if batting over the obviousness of it all. He followed up, nodding further encouragement as matter-of-fact as if he'd only been giving engine advice.

'Is that a common part of going ashore?' I asked.

'Depends on the shore, really, and who's aboard. Second time I sailed round the world I took my daughter, Jana. The rules then were straight: no women allowed. I did a lot more partying like that when I sailed round on my first boat, on *Lady Jay*.' He gave a shake of the head, sighed with good times. 'Ahh yeah.'

'You sailed around the world with your daughter?'

My whole face must have smiled, came reflected back in Laurie's.

'I did. And I tell you it's an amazing thing for a child. She used to be up in the crow's nest,' Laurie glowed with nostalgia, held out his arms, 'and I used to take her by the ankles, over the side so that she could clean barnacles off the bottom with the broom. Then there was the time when she was diving, and I was below her in the water as a whale swam right by and breached the surface. Ah yeah, some of the times we had.'

'How long were you at sea together?'

He paused thoughtfully, then smacked his lips at the memory. 'Must have been about five years, all told.'

Laurie gave a wave of the hand, beckoning me below deck. In the cramped space that served as his galley kitchen, navigation table and bedroom, Laurie pointed up to the topmost of the wooden panels that formed the wall of the room. From thick, wooden frames, two young girls looked out. He pointed to one, fair-haired and smiling.

'That's Camilla. We were gonna call her "Julian" but when she came out she had a pair of flaps instead of a pair of balls!'

Laurie gave his foghorn laugh, his hand moving right, voice settling with the softness that comes for a person they are happy to love but sad to miss.

'And that's Jana.'

I looked at the photo of the girl: dark hair and eyes, an intensity of expression, determined, a strong and unbroken eyebrow across her forehead. The whole face had a look of defiance to it, and of features that were not only Western.

'They've got the same mother?'

Laurie shook his head. 'Jana's mother was Polynesian. She was beautiful, mate, but she drank too much. So in the end I brought Jana up pretty much alone.'

'You have other kids?'

'Five. With different mothers though. I've got four girls, then a son I've never met.'

'Where's he?'

Laurie's voice grew pensive. 'Norway, I think. I'm not sure he knows his father's out here and, yer know, would like to know him. We've never met. I tried to make contact but he didn't seem interested. I had him with a Filipino woman I met in Manila.'

'You still in contact?'

'Nuh uh. When we lost touch, and I thought she might be pregnant, I tried to find her in the city, but she'd left. I felt awful that I might've gotten a Filipino girl pregnant, 'cos those guys in the Philippines are something crazy with their Catholicism, and outside of marriage, I didn't want her turfed out on her ear by her family, with nobody to support her. I went to the suburb of Manila she came from, and I got a small notice photocopied, saying I was looking for her. I started giving it out everywhere and eventually a woman in a hairdresser's came out to me while I was handing the things out, and mentioned something about another town, and that fit with something she'd said once about relatives there. So I thought to myself, "Ah right, she's OK. She'll be OK."'

I considered how much a half-century had changed the nature of communication, how easy it had become to find people briefly encountered and then parted from by different courses in life. In my imagination there appeared a younger Laurie, patiently walking the tangled streets of Manila in an effort to do the decent thing by a girl he'd got pregnant, like some resolute human search engine for a friend set to one day become only memory. Laurie, as in all things, was a paradox; a mixture of one who knew how to be a rogue but always had in him an eternal sentimentality, a desire to do right by people and stay dignified. It always amused me too, that a man who would sometimes talk in terms of 'stock' and the purity of race, had been led by his indiscriminate love of a good time to do fine work in adding a half-dozen mixed lives to the beautiful genetic mongrel that was the human race. That was just Laurie, I would learn. The ideas in his head were only ideas, and while I would never agree with them, I knew they were only that. In front of him, before his eyes, he only ever saw people.

He put his palms to his knees and pushed himself up, stepping quietly past where Nim lay spread out and resting. I moved back above deck, and watched as Laurie went down towards the stove, returning with the wooden handle of the kettle held in his hand, and two mugs hooked by a finger, resting together.

'Want some green tea, Jules?'

'Sure. I can't sleep anyway.'

Laurie sprinkled some leaf into the mugs, then filled them to a little below the brim, steam winding upwards as the dry leaf unfurled in the hot water. He took a large jam jar from the shelf, holding a thick-set substance a colour halfway between yellow and orange. With the end of a knife, Laurie prised out a small wedge of it and stirred it into his tea.

'That honey?'

'Syrup.'

He sipped at the tea and handed me my cup. I picked up the knife, adding a little of the congealed, crystallised substance to my own.

'Syrup from the coconut palm. You run a tap into the tree, have to keep cutting at the bark every half hour, because the sap has a coagulant in it. And, if you ferment that for just half an hour, you get *tooba*!'

'Tooba?'

'Tooba's a mild narcotic. And it make you so happy, Jules. There are islands in Micronesia where the natives all take it, and you can go and take it with them and just chill out together. But, once a month, they have a ferry taking supplies to the island' – Laurie's face became suddenly very grave – 'and on the boat they'll have whisky and spirits to trade.'

'That's bad?'

'People end up murdered, Jules! The natives'll take tooba all their lives without a worry, but give 'em whisky and they turn real nasty. All they want to do is fight.'

'Feels like drink is quite a problem out here in general.'

'You betchya. Not just for the natives either, the whites are even worse. People come out to the tropics, and if you've a thirst for beer, or if things ain't so good, you just drink to take the edge off the heat. For years you don't even get drunk, mate, it's so hot your body just processes it instantly. A few of the guys I know now out here, now they're starting to get drunk, it's starting to affect them, and that tells you they can't process it any more, their bodies have started breaking down inside.'

'Are there many other drugs going around?'

'Yeah. They've always been about. I guess drugs were a big part of anything if you were young in the sixties. When we were diving for abalone, and when we weren't working, we used to take a wrap of acid and put it in your dive buddy's mouthpiece when he came back up to the boat. Then you'd send him back down to the fish and the coral.' Laurie laughed loud. 'The colours, Jules, the colours down there! Ahh fuck yeah, it was a mess. Most of that sort of fun I had was when I was sailing around the world on *Lady Jay*. When I was on *Atlanta*, with Jana, it was all really clean living. I never got into it all, the drugs and what have you, like a lot of guys did. I'm glad I never did any heroin, because I know I've got an addictive side. That would've been the end of me.'

'There was a lot of it out here?'

'Ah yeah. There was one time, a few of us drunk and high and all half-passed out on deck. One guy, I forget his name but he was a nasty piece of work. He'd been on heroin a long time and came up to me with a syringe pricked and ready to go. I still remember his eyes, they were small and yellow like two pissholes in the snow, and he came towards me with the syringe saying, "and this one's for you, Laurie," and I thought to myself, the hell it is, and I told him to back right off.'

Laurie paused for reflection, then turned with a purpose, in that way he did when making an important point about himself that needed to be heard.

'Some parts of my life there were more drugs, some parts less. I don't need 'em, but when they're around that was fine by me. Obviously there wasn't any of that shit when Jana was on board.'

With that point stressed, a story took hold of him again.

'Sailing round the world in *Lady Jay*, first time crossing the Atlantic I put down anchor at this small jetty, and I didn't know where the hell I was, only that it was South Carolina somewhere. So I takes myself ashore and walked into a bar, and it was a bar for blacks ... and every head looked round at my little white face, and I hadn't seen anyone at all for weeks. I reckon that it might've turned nasty, but as soon as I opened my mouth and they heard I was a foreigner, that was all right and we had a drink together. They were good guys, and one of them worked the grounds of some local big shot, plantation owner … Greenfield Plantation I think it was called. He asked me where I was from and I told him Australia, so he said I had to go with him back to the manor house. And staying there was Julia Lindsay, the daughter of Norman Lindsay.'

'I don't know who that is.'

'Norman Lindsay was a famous Australian artist, did a lot of illustrations – nymphs and other mystical stuff – and his daughter had hooked up with this plantation guy, tobacco and cotton, worth a fortune. Inman was his name, Walker Inman. He died just the other year, and Julia Lindsay, she was bored as hell there. That groundsman thought she'd like the Australian company so they took me back and when they did, I remember Inman coming out to meet me dressed in a linen suit, shaking my hand with a big drink in the other. Ah fuck, Jules, that guy was out of his head the whole time I was there, and he came right up and leans over and welcomes me, says, "Make yourself at home, sir. We'll get you a room fixed up; have whatever you want to drink, and you can help yourself to all the cocaine you want.'

Laurie smiled. 'I stayed two weeks.'

Confrontations – morning

A breakfast of bananas and papaya began the day, with its trail of yellow and orange peels and rinds floating away until they were taken by fish or eventually grew saturated with water and sank, waving down towards the seabed. The smoke of Surin's fires could be seen, with another slow plume coming up from the rubbish heap, and each smouldering fire lifting to build a haze at either end of the beachfront. From a tree on a small island, close to where we had moored and little more than a few large rocks and undergrowth, a bird screeched loud at the presence of *Atlanta*. The silhouette of its large beak opened wide into a sickle-like curve, as its yellow breast heaved in the air for another new call. Black wings spread, and with two beats of their span, a white underside took effortlessly to the sky. On a chopping board lay the shining steel of the cleaver, a fly moving down its blade, greedy for the grease of rancid chicken guts painted on to the metal. The smell of vegetable oil lingered from the galley, and the caramelised remains of the fried pumpkin stuck in charred debris to the hotplate.

Nim stepped on to the deck, looking around and shaking her head at the sight as she walked with her weight heavily on her heels. She gathered a few plates, talking to herself before putting them aside and sitting down with a cup of water.

'Clean up, before go to island, Nim have to clean up. Nim good wife, have to do everything.' She laughed to herself. 'Here have to look after boat and on island have to speak with people for television. Always working.'

From afar came the call of another bird, at which Nim startled a little. 'Loud bird,' she said to herself and Laurie swung in his hammock, putting his fingers to his temple, giving it a gentle, circular rub.

'All right, all right, Nim. If you could just give me twenty minutes without talking would ya, darling? I can't hear myself think up here.'

'Twenty minutes?' Nim's neck craned forward, brow furrowed.

'Yeah. That OK, darling?'

'OK, Laulie.' She smiled at the ease of the instruction. 'I love you. Twenty minutes.'

And I listened as they said their sort of temporary goodbye for twenty minutes, with Laurie in his hammock and Nim watching the sea next to him. Somehow, on those terms halfway between romance and pragmatics, their relationship managed to work really rather well.

A little while later, a large speedboat came gliding up to us; its sides sheer, shut away and menacing beside the sails, masts, ropes and open face of *Atlanta*. The motors slowed and a wake fell wide and deep behind it. From a glass door, a leg in jackboots appeared and a man stepped out, noticeably Thai rather than Moken in appearance, dressed in green combat trousers and a dark green polo shirt. He put hands on hips as the boat moved up alongside *Atlanta*. Laurie came up from the galley, the sound of motors slowing to a reserved but steady throb.

'Ah, fuck. We've got niggers coming.'

The word hit me; not quite understanding at who or why it was being used.

'Park rangers, looking for money, from us. Always, from people like us while the fucking trawlers are out there killing the sea.'

'I guess they need to pay wages, keep out poachers, that sort of thing,' I reasoned.

'We're not troubling anyone here. It's the sea, the damn sea, and it's our boat, and still we've gotta pay for it, just to be here!'

The boat came up alongside and an inflatable was dropped overboard to cushion it as it docked right up against *Atlanta*'s hull. Laurie went up to the rail with his hands on his hips, reflecting the stance of the ranger back at him, the two of them with their chests out.

'What do you want?' was all Laurie asked, simple as you like, speaking straight English as if it was the responsibility of the ranger to understand him.

'National Park Ticket.' The ranger sounded uncertain, only doing his job, kind of a quiver to his voice.

'What for?'

'For mooring.'

The ranger swallowed hard. Laurie stared at him.

'How much?'

The ranger held up some fingers, gave an apologetic look.

I saw then that in Laurie you had the trickle-down of Empire. His passport, bound in battered red, allowed him to show up on any beach or quay he desired, and it permitted his journey in any waters. To ensure it seldom came to that, his white skin – no matter how tanned it had become – meant that few ever doubted his rigid but informal rank within the world, situated at the top of its hierarchy. The language he spoke, and others heard, as if they should have understood it before he was expected to understand theirs, no matter the naval borders in which *Atlanta* floated. Laurie withdrew, went below deck and on coming back up, a few bills changed hands. The ranger gave a short bow of relieved gratitude which Laurie, having successfully asserted his displeasure with the situation, returned respectfully as the man stepped back over to his own boat, retrieving the inflatable and neatly pulling away from us. I watched the speedboat move off as Laurie reclined back to his hammock. I had to say something.

'Why'd you call him a nigger anyway? You can't call people that.'

'What's that, Jules?' Laurie looked up, his attention caught, as if I'd simply asked something about a cup of tea.

'"Nigger" … he's not even black, and even if he was, it's not right to call people that.'

'You get niggers in all colours, Jules. Black, white, slopehead.'

'What's a "slopehead"?' I interrupted, confused.

'Chinese.' Laurie didn't so much as break stride in his sentence. 'And there's a white guy from Skegness, living on Ko Lipi, who tried to have me removed from the marina once, and hands down he's the worst nigger in Thailand.' Laurie laughed, counting them off on his fingers and rising in crescendo. 'Then there's no allowing for Frenchmen, Arabs, never trust the damn Swiss, the Dutch are a handful, you've gotta be careful with the Germans ... and most of all, always watch out for prejudiced people!'

He laughed again as he said that, and I never would be totally sure if he was only being ironic. I returned to the original subject.

'So, what, a *nigger* is anyone you don't like?'

'Yeah, something like that.'

'But it's still disrespectful, especially to black people.'

Laurie grew affronted at that, leant forwards a little in his hammock, his feelings seemingly hurt.

'Look, Jules, when I was growing up there was nothing wrong with calling a black person that. And they'd call themselves that too, and they still do. I don't know why you'd be so concerned about it.'

'Because I think people are pretty much the same, and it's stupid to make a difference out of skin colour, especially if people are offended by a word.'

'Some slopehead in Malaysia ripped me off a thousand dollars for some cans of linseed oil the other month, just because he could. You've gotta look after yourself, Jules. I tell you, the Chinese in particular ... they think they're superior. You should see them with the Thai, like they're servants or something. Packs of Chinese, in a group, and not an individual among 'em. They're all raised with the thought that they're from the greatest country on earth, I reckon it's probably only the Illuminati among the Chinese that are actually individuals at all.'

I looked on, my face unmoved by his reasoning.

'I'm telling ya, Jules. This, it's just the way of the world.'

Sensing that we weren't about to see eye to eye, I wandered off to the other end of the boat. It wasn't the last time we'd cross one another's views on such a subject, and those conversations between Laurie and me perhaps joined in a loud discourse between generations, one that around that time was coming to surface the world over. Younger people who'd mostly grown up with no concern for skin colour, religion or sexual persuasion, struggled at relationships with older people we cared about and respected, all the while sure that many of their views were products of a history that had amplified human differences rather than similarities. Perhaps in the elderly those prejudices could seem harmless enough, dying out, but I worried what would happen when they were picked up and transmitted to individuals who still had sufficient energy and years to try and shape the world in the mould of such ideas.

A further thought would go on troubling me. Laurie's talents and his sense of adventure meant he had fulfilled a life's need for adversity using the elements; the brilliance of star-riddled skies and the great waves of entire oceans. Back home, in sterile cities and uneventful suburbs, I feared for the fate of human minds without such vast and glorious canvasses, and such pure challenges, on which to sketch their meanings of life.

In all the time we spent together, it was a contrast that would never let up: the hard words from Laurie's mouth, and the dislocation between them and his warm disposition towards all who came his way. I thought of the world's discriminations; where bombs were dropped on foreign cities and the poor had their right to farm a little land bought up by corporations, where oceans were trawled dry of fish and nomadic people forbidden to move because of national borders that disregarded the traditions that came before them. All of that was racism. I felt sure that it was those hard, physical structures that destroyed people and cultures, sowing division where there was no need of it. In skyscrapers and cities around the world, it was easy for polite, smartly dressed scoundrels to make racism the prevail of

an old man living on a boat. We were all guilty of our own prejudices, the contents of our own thoughts, but Laurie was a drifter who
had never harmed nor wielded power over anyone else – could mere
words, offensive or not, be held responsible for such great injustices?
Like many, he had failed to unlearn many of the prejudices he'd
been raised with; it took a special human to be able to do that, and
I suppose Laurie was special in other ways. That particular talent, he
struggled with.

Across that week, I think I came to a conclusion that our world
was made of twin systems: one of ideas and the other of physical
acts. The problem was that where the culture of ideas was polluted,
where they discriminated between one life or way of life as more
valuable than another, so would unscrupulous people – whether
politicians in suits or thugs on streets – begin to act on the basis of
those ideas. I was sure that Laurie had a sense of self, and of human
instincts, strong enough to keep the ideas distinct from the real, but
not everyone possessed that disposition. He had lived among people
of all faiths and colours, those who attached hooks to their skin in
tribal ritual or used pigs as currency. I trusted that the diversity of
his experience meant that he knew, on a deeper level, that all of his
caricatures were only that, caricatures; self-preserving views ready to
be modified for the next person met, of whatever race. Despite his
stubbornness, there was no prejudice in him that would not melt to
warmth at a smiling face, no matter how different from his own. He
spoke politely of few and yet had time of day for anyone. Perhaps you
think he simply became a friend to me, that I became someone who
grew inclined to make excuses for him … you wouldn't be wrong.

Juy – midday

Back on the beachfront, the crew reassembled and ready to interview, Chief found us faster than we could find him. Since our arrival he'd seemed to keep a distant watch on us, just in case Reinard might have returned with more liquor for the bottle he had by then drunk dry. Seeing us making our way towards him, Chief came back out and made it his business to shorten our journey. Stumbling a little, suffused with the whiff of bourbon, he shook my hand in a firm grip, then moved his hand to my forearm and leered.

His eyes had turned blood red by then, and he put forwards a palm. 'Money, money!' he called, while under his other arm were the last precious vapours, and the dear memory, of the empty bottle he held like a comfort blanket.

Nim faced him, her chin proudly forward, and spoke in Thai; asking his willingness to talk about Moken ways of life, and the organisation of the community he was nominally the head of.

Chief's eyes scrunched up tight in puzzlement, his nostrils flared quickly with an intake of breath, the man so unsure what she was getting at that Nim might as well have been talking to him in English. She turned to me and shook her head.

'He drunk. I think he have nothing to say.'

Reinard interjected. 'Perhaps a few words?'

Nim looked back, stoney-faced. 'He drunk, he can't talk proper.'

Reinard looked round forlornly in search of a second opinion. Jake shook his head.

There was, it was safe to say, no circumstance in which after a few moments of contemplation even Reinard could conceive of recording Chief as evidence of traditional Moken life. One bit of benevolent cultural imperialism that could probably have done with being left preserved where Moken were concerned was the idea that indigenous peoples should not be given alcohol. I looked down the beach at Reinard, who had by then taken to pacing the shore pensively. On one level, Chief's high rank and lack of manners made him thoroughly dislikeable, but on another, he was just an alcoholic, and – more than that – an alcoholic that our own showing up, and presumably the appearance of farang before us, had recklessly enabled. For those few days that we came to know him, Chief seemed not so pleasant a character; a man uncaring and aloof from his community. And yet, inebriated with alcohol, or else recovering and hungover, it was clear he himself could not really be blamed. Chief was only a victim.

More telling than his alcoholism, however, and in a community stripped of any but society's most elemental trimmings, Chief was as great a lesson as you could ever find to demonstrate the injustice of hereditary privilege. Of all the Moken, and having done nothing but being born to earn his status, Chief was the only one ever to seem the least dishonourable, with the exception of his closest aides – if 'aides' was the right word for them. They alone had disappeared – quick and selfish – with the gift of bourbon Reinard had given them. They alone had asked for money, grabbing at a wrist or arm in an act of appeasement when they sensed they had angered you with their pushiness. Unlike the rest of the Moken, they alone seemed to do no work at all. Chief himself lived in a larger hut at the end of the beach, and from through its open door you could see a music system including a pair of large speakers. In the setting of a beachfront village, with a generator that ran only three hours a day to provide light in the evenings, the presence of that system appeared like a great luxury; the equivalent of a swimming pool in suburbia. In a wealthy country with a population in the tens of millions, the pageantry of royals could be disguised as only pomp and tradition; but within the scarcity of Surin, where Chief had an abundant sense of entitlement but few means by which to satisfy it, the arrangement was glaringly ugly.

Gathered at the far end of the village, with Chief's media career already over, we discussed a plan for the day's filming. Erik stood off to one side, arms folded and kicking at the sand, while Reinard pointed out to the bay at low tide. Lines of *kabang* leaned over to one side where they were pulled up and moored upon the long, seaweed-covered ropes that sliced through the beach. Nim paced up and down, impatient.

'I think we should get more sailing footage.' Reinard extended his hands to hoist a sail, miming his idea to Nim. 'Something like, you know, a Moken in the traditional *kabang*. Maybe one with the sailing mast, or perhaps rowing.'

It was a new idea, one not previously discussed, and Jake looked upwards as if considering its merits.

'We could. But I haven't seen anyone using them.'

Reinard leaned in at him, pointing in a moment of abracadabra.

'Exactly, they don't use them any more! But that is the traditional boat here, the one the older generation used. We should try and preserve that tradition by recording a little of it.'

By and large I'd watched Jake duck the eccentricities of Reinard's ideas. The guy did largely as he was told and held back, hiding behind his cameras: sometimes he would dictate quietly where they were pointed, away from Reinard's wilder suggestions, or he would exaggerate a technical issue to suggest something was impossible, rather than engaging with the most fanciful whims that went thrown his way. On this occasion, though, Jake winced.

'It's a nice idea, but.' He waited a moment for the words, put a palm to his face. 'I dunno. If what we're trying to get is the real Moken way of life, I'm not sure it makes sense filming someone in a boat nobody uses any more.'

Reinard's mouth opened, preparing a defence of traditional wisdom and sailing craft, but as he did so a stranger came shuffling towards us. The attention of our group shifted towards the newcomer. Slow and hunkered, a crippled figure neared, his body leaning heavily on a crutch with plastic armrests and the metal uprights spotted with corrosion. In the rigid right angles of his handicap, braced between crutch and limb, the man walked out from the forest, awkwardly supporting his twisted body, and coming steadily into view with a smile filled by such life and grace that defied his wrecked frame.

He gave a laugh as he saw us, as if he too realised what a ridiculous crew we were. His light brown skin was crowned by grey and black hair that fell straight to dark eyes, steadily disappearing and lightening with the thick, sallow-coloured husks of cataracts. Up close, the man's gaze seemed to stare very nearly straight through us. His skin was scarred in many places; dark purple with older wounds, a pink lashing from what looked like it must have come from an encounter with a jellyfish. His shoulder was twisted, with a ball of cartilage protruding from the joint and stuck tight within a wrap of skin that seemed to have had the pigment forced out of it by whatever grew there. His arm sat, bending back on itself, and the old man's kneecaps faced one another as if looking to the other for support. One of his feet stuck perpendicular from the rest of his body and, as a whole, the figure folded in and out on itself like a half-finished work of origami. From his knee hung the ends of a dirty, stained muslin fabric, the medical rag clinging to a deep wound that wept yellow pus from inside a wide ring of red blood and skin stripped of half its layers. Kneeling a little, Jake pointed to it with a concerned expression, to which the man just laughed and hit his forehead as if in condemnation of his own clumsiness. In a high, singing voice and with a smile that missed one front tooth, he replied, as Nim squatted down beside him to take a closer look.

'He say he fell over.' And she gestured a tipping motion with her wrist. 'He say he pour petrol on it yesterday. Soon will be OK.'

And that was Juy.

That old petrol disinfectant trick was one more gem of indigenous knowledge that scuppered Reinard's romance about the ways of the Moken. In some respects, truth be told, Juy summed up neatly the limitations of any mysticism about what passed for daily life among the community. Juy had the bends, almost to a point at which you might more accurately have said that the bends had Juy; it held him captive in his own body for however long his hard but happy, grudgeless life was due to last. Keeping to his pace, we walked back along the beach to his hut, and the thick nails and slightly twisting fingers of the Moken man's hand held at the steadying rest of Reinard's proffered arm. The withering of his body, though more extreme than most, was in itself nothing so remarkable for a Moken dive man, and Reinard and Laurie had both mentioned the dangers of the bends. Juy spoke slowly, Nim repeating shortened versions of his long and excitable sentences in which he, no different to any old man, relived the stories of his glory days for any newcomer willing to listen.

'He say when he was young he was one of the best divers of all the men, on Phuket or Surin. All his life he say he work underwater.'

With all respect to Juy, it was strange too, to know the science of his disfiguration, the actual causes, better than he did himself. Juy and the Moken knew that he suffered from a sickness incurred from the sea, generally from too much time beneath the sea, and specifically as a result of one incident in which the engine of an air compressor aboard the boat he dived from had broken, so that it no longer pressed oxygen down the hose and into Juy's mask as he walked on the seabed collecting pearls. With the motor at a halt, he had been left without any air in his lungs, shooting back to the surface as fast as his legs could kick and arms could pull him.

In as much as that, we all shared a common opinion of what exactly had happened to Juy. Our specific understanding, however, diverged from there – the science of the bends was of no relevance on Surin. Juy did not need to know the details of the increasing pressure a body was required to withstand as it went deeper below water, forcing more gases into that body than they took in at the surface. With the air pumped from the surface containing four times as much nitrogen as oxygen, underwater those particles grew ever smaller under pressure, and so allowed still more nitrogen gases to enter the man's body. The result was that the cartilage of Juy's joints had slowly filled with all the accumulated nitrogen, leaving hardened knots of dense gas that would not have time to dissipate and leave the body if they returned too fast to the surface pressure above the water. While a gradual return from the depths he'd reached would have allowed the gases to equalise back to normal, in spending a whole lifetime below water, or shooting once, fast, up towards the shimmering sun, Juy had been all but guaranteed to face the crippling that eventually set in.

Juy, for his part, thought the bends no more than a case of bad luck and bad spirits. More incense may well have sorted it, a few garlands of flowers hanging round the neck of a spiritual icon. He knew his condition had stemmed from his life beneath the sea, and that fateful day in particular, and perhaps that knowledge alone meant it was immaterial what else he understood of it – the rest was mere detail. Still, there was a strangeness in understanding the composition of another man's injury more intimately than he did himself. Naturally, there was also a fix for the misfortune Juy had suffered that day, and around the coastal cities and islands of Southeast Asia were dotted a dozen or so decompression chambers; places where farang divers could be rushed in an emergency at the first signs of the bends, when headaches and a tingling of skin set in, and often when diving after heavy drinking meant their bodies were oxygen-depleted through alcohol. These chambers would artificially return the body to its underwater pressure and then gradually bring it back to surface pressure, relieving the body of the accumulated nitrogen so as to restore the full potential of a Western life back home. The owners of the chambers must have been turning a steady profit from the certainty that the farang – whether by insurance payout or their own pockets – would stump up for the full restoration of their health but for a stiff headache.

For Juy and the Moken, just like the details of the bends itself, decompression chambers might as well not have existed at all. Health was a luxury for those with money; decompression sickness belonged in a world of rich people and, as was evident, Juy could make do with rust-spattered crutches. As we greeted him, the full reality of his life and what its sad story meant to us hit immediately home. Juy would make for a fantastic interview.

Nim translated our request, Juy consented gladly. We followed him back to his hut, hanging behind a little, so as to film him hobbling home, and build a little context for his story. The hut was a sorry affair, and with the arm he didn't need to hold his crutch, he lifted a washing line and made his way towards the porch at the front. Reinard disappeared with a small camera that had been mounted on an old coat-hanger bracket, a thing he came to grow fond of. Wandering wild and free, wearing a baseball cap to keep the sun from his blue eyes, Reinard roamed the area to capture additional material that would intersperse the interview. Meanwhile, Jake and I perused the setting.

'We probably need somewhere a bit sad for the background,' I suggested.

Jake nodded. 'Yeah. No flowers.'

We skirted the perimeter, made towards the back of the hut, where an old plastic barrel and a coil of pipe sat beside small pools of mud. A low step was made from a battered, rotting piece of wood, placed across two bricks at uneven heights. We pointed, Nim translated. Hoisting the sarong of yellow-red chequers that he wore around his middle, Juy sat down on the step, his knees up in front of him, just beneath the line of his ever-present smile. Over his shoulder was the slumped metal frame of a sorry-looking camp bed, a weave of fabric for its sleeping surface, and the room unkempt and full of shadows. It was perfect.

We set up and, through Nim, gave Juy his orders: 'Nim's voice will be edited out in the final film, so answer in sentences that include her questions because the audience won't hear her voice asking them. Speak Moken. Don't look at the camera, pretend the camera isn't there.'

Juy nodded an understanding, still smiling, and began to speak for the camera in Moken. Later he repeated those words to Nim in Thai, and those words were relayed finally to us, completing a laborious process with meaning lost at every stage, in a broken English.

'From the sea we get many things, and because we are poor, the sea feeds us.' He held up bent fingers, beginning uncertainly to count on them. 'It feeds us with fish, but also with things that we can sell. It feeds us with sea cucumbers.' Juy imitated the crawling of a sea creature with his hands. 'We find pearls and from them we make money for our families.' He paused, long and thoughtful, his head lifted upwards and eyes shining. 'Thai boats always have at least one Moken man with them, because Thai do not know sea like Moken. Nobody know the sea like Moken know the sea.' Juy smiled proudly, rising with a gentle superiority as he pointed the hardened skin of an arthritic, stick-like finger, right up close to a cataract. 'Thai do not know how to *look*. They do not know the waters, the islands. They do not know that a fish will not bite anything from a cold hook. They do not know that there are streams of fresh water that come out from some rocks under the sea,' and Juy smiled with his eyes, but his mouth moved slow as he cupped his hands beneath it, 'and you can drink from those streams, and the water there is so good, so cool and fresh.'

We left him to pause a while, without a question, the camera still rolling so as to capture that uncertain moment where a face comes over a little vulnerable; not sure if the silence is because the speaker has somehow performed badly, erred, let us down. That moment, that wide-eyed moment where the subject swallows hard with doubt; that always looks good. Juy was doing just great. We moved on.

'How old are you?'

He laughed, and in that man you knew there was no grievance against the hand life had dealt him.

'I do not know!'

He laughed more, covering his eyes in disbelief, as if the question itself were either immodest or ludicrous.

'They say that I am fifty-eight, but I cannot be fifty-eight. If I was, I would be wiser.'

Juy looked every day of fifty-eight, and then some. Mortality was building in his features, worn at by a harder life than the point of history he'd been born into should have left him. We got to the chase, the payload, that moment that would really make the interview work the audience.

'Can you tell us about your last dive, your accident?'

He nodded, already understood that this was important to us, and somehow didn't judge us for it. In fairness, and hapless though the execution was, there was nobody among that crew who wanted anything but the best for Juy and the Moken. It was simply implicit that to achieve that, whatever *that* was, would involve at least some confessional tales of hardship. The goal was to get hardship down on camera and hope the watching eyes back home were not yet wholly desensitised, that they could still be moved by one more instance of injustice and adversity elsewhere in the world. Juy kicked us off.

'I don't remember how many years ago it was. I was diving' – he waved out to sea – 'in a place that was new to me. In a place that was very deep. I dived on the end of the pipe.' He made a fist, and put it to his lips and breathed through it loudly, his chest rising. 'And as I walked along the floor of the sea, I felt the air slowing down, and then the air stopped, and then' – Juy looked right at us, as if drunk with the thought – 'I could not breathe.'

Motionless, a line of us stood behind the camera, watching the old man recite the story of how he had become maimed. He pulled his hands over his waistline.

'We always take a bag when we go diving.'

Juy looked around and saw a plastic bag on the ground. He picked it up, dusted it free of sand and blew into it so that the thing inflated. He trapped the air inside with a satisfied demonstration of the method he would have been using, and held the bag tight to his middle.

'And we have the bag on our belt for emergency if the air stops.' He moved the bag to his mouth. 'I take it and breathe some air, slowly, while I swim as quick as can back to surface.'

Juy lifted his nose up in the only look of disdain or negativity he ever made. 'Now, the men dive with two bags for spare air. Two!'

Juy shook his head. 'In my time it was only one. And one was enough!'

He looked on in irritation, as if health and safety neurosis had ruined the tradition he had grown up with. Meanwhile, his withered body leaned forward, the crutch beside him as if an exhibit of evidence for the usefulness of those precautions, and so many more besides an extra plastic bag, that Juy seemed to judge unnecessary.

'That day I swim up to the surface, breathing my bag, and I keep going up and the sun is very big.' Juy threw away the bag and instead spread his palms. 'And all the sea is very bright with the sun, even when still very deep. And I keep going.' He kicked his twisted legs at the sand below his step. 'And finally the water stops' – he gave a gasping breath of air – 'and I am next to the boat, and I can breathe.'

He paused a while, then gave a dismissive wave and even a giggle, as if the whole turn of events wasn't so bad really.

'At first I was OK. Maybe for a day I was OK. And then my head hurts, more and more. And slowly, this happens to me. My leg stops working, and my arms stop working. My hands. Stop working.'

He smiled at us, shrugged again, wondering if all that was what we had wanted. He sat there, in front of the line of us: the camera lens, Erik large over my shoulder with a microphone hovering just above Juy's head, Reinard holding the little coat-hanger bracket for his own camera. Jake hit a button to stop recording, then made a slight noise of unpleasant surprise.

'OK. We might have to do that last bit again. My memory card ran out.'

Real Pros – afternoon

Later that afternoon, Juy set us up. Filming underwater, capturing the Moken in their habitat beneath the sea, had for a while loomed large in Reinard's visualisation of his otherwise unplanned masterpiece. After his accident, Juy had been given a *kabang* of his own by the combined goodwill of the community and Thai authorities; a rudimentary payment of disability support so that able-bodied men could give him a small fee for use of his boat, a means of production that he owned and they did not. Reinard, you could feel as Juy's story developed, was starting to grow more and more set on the diving scenes; the man had a tendency to seize on one idea at a time, and suddenly that notion of an underwater world with the Moken within it defined everything for him. Quietly he ruminated aloud that funds were running short, but money was no object with material like this, and so with Juy's help in administering the deal, he agreed to drop the Moken a few thousand baht for the trouble of taking us out in the boat, with a waterproof camera to descend beneath the sea. With the Moken banned by national park conservation laws from netting any more than a few fish at a time, and prohibited from trading what they caught, when the money changed hands there was no doubting it – we'd been their best catch in years.

The deal was twofold: we wanted a few scenes of the traditional spear fishing, with a free-diving Moken man swimming unaided through the depths in order to demonstrate their apparent gift for holding their breath beneath water. After that, we wanted footage of a man diving on the end of the hose, the hookah. The motor on the deck of a *kabang* would pump a compressor, sending air down to the Moken man with a belt of weights, walking on the seabed, scouring for pearls or other pickings the Moken used to try and pay their way with in this world. If they found nothing, no problem, so long as the footage looked the part. The first would be a traditional, pastoral version of life at sea; the second, a vision of decrepit and ragtag machinery, how the power of petrol and industry was enlisted in a daily struggle to survive.

Back on *Atlanta* we waited, readying kit as a team of five Moken appeared in a *kabang*, the propellor behind them chopping at the sea and moving them towards us. Those guys knew exactly what to do. My guess was that they'd been here before; they knew just how to go about hitting up a camera crew for a good day's wages. Fishing for media must have been safer and more lucrative than anything left on their sea floor, and as they neared, a man standing in a commanding pose upon the bow called over. Pointing around the back of *Atlanta*, he shouted out to Nim.

'He say do you want to film them sailing past the boat?'

Jake grabbed a tripod. 'Yes! Actually that'd be great.'

And Nim gave an enthusiastic nod as she called back, so that the pilot turned the propellor to a new angle and the *kabang* arced wide around us to make the pass. I watched as each of those Moken looked solemnly out to sea, just as you'd expect from a band of humble fishermen who belonged in another world; a tropics beyond thought of trade or media. Those guys knew the drill: real stoic, well aware not to look at the camera, they did a wide and meaningless U-turn, then came back alongside for us to climb aboard. One called again up to Nim.

'Did that look OK? You want them to do again?'

Somewhere between indigenous wisdom and none-too-shabby film producers, they looked over at us and waited for an answer. We had no complaints.

All aboard their *kabang*, Erik and Laurie remaining with *Atlanta*, our cameras rolled. Five Moken gathered at one end, while at the other there huddled three white blokes and Nim crouching behind a lens, its barrel peerless black and trained right on the Moken.

Capturing the moment, *shooting* a scene, the language of it all was as martial as the act, and armed with those cameras we engaged our warfare for eyes and souls back home. The Moken threw any Western-looking belongings … the camera cases, the rucksacks, anything that gave any hint of an orderly world … right out of the frame, even put an old cloth over some of it. They stowed the spare microphones in a small hole under the seat; the buoyancy jacket went down there too, along with a camera bag, even the case for Reinard's sunglasses and a few other tiny oddments that might easily have escaped the notice of those less thorough. No stone was left unturned and those guys were proving pretty well-adapted to the new age coming after all: how to take a traditional boat full of Moken men and a film crew and make it look like only a traditional boat full of Moken men.

The engine coughed up sea as it took us out into the Andaman; distant enough to be out of sight of *Atlanta* and land, not so far that the journey would inconvenience anyone for longer than we'd paid for. Reinard reiterated his disappointment at the motor, mounted on the rear of the *kabang* and the exhaust stack protruding from it. He pointed to its carburettor and exposed valves, chambers and coils of smoke-blackened steel, then touched politely at Nim's shoulder.

'Can you ask why people don't sail now, the traditional way?'

Nim translated some words. The Moken man on the pole of the tiller spoke, shrugged and scratched his head a little as Nim turned back to us.

'He say petrol is easy.'

Once in position, Jake readied the waterproof camera into a plastic housing that would take it down below. From where they had been hidden out of frame, he lifted fins, goggles, a small oxygen tank, a buoyancy jacket and a breathing regulator for himself. Opposite him, two Moken spat into the glass face of large, sealed visors that fitted over their nose and eyes, wiping clean the surface and making sure the hose that fed into the side of the mask was securely connected.

Another two men waited at the rear of the boat, one eating at a slice of melon and the other leaning on the tiller beside the metal face of the engine, gleaming with sunlight. A final man lifted the compressor into position and Jake again filmed the scene inside the boat while the rest of us crouched at his feet so as not to intrude on the camera's line of sight. The man in charge of the compressor started it up, so that it shuddered into life with a foul belch of black smoke, and he waited for Jake to lower his camera before giving a thumbs-up that all was ready to go. Jake returned the thumbs-up, and the two Moken dropped over the side of the boat, while the man on the compressor began feeding out the lines of hose as they drifted deeper down beneath our boat. Holding the camera inside its transparent housing, Jake dropped in after them, and with only the noise of the compressor for company, we all waited.

The waves around the boat settled; the last of the divers' disappearing bubbles coming to an end as their helper kept feeding the hose overboard, down towards whatever might be happening beneath us. Reinard leant far over the side with his own camera on its coat hanger, lowering it to just above the surface to capture a view of the very point where sea met horizon. Leaning back into the boat, he pulled his shorts higher up his thighs, turned to me and spoke with a determined voice so innocent it was hard not to admire.

'We need to save this way of life.'

For all that he was well-meaning, and against my wishes, I found myself cringing a little. It was as if Reinard had forgotten that the only way of life we were currently engaged with was one we'd paid to have recreated for film. Whether or not it conferred many advantages on the Moken the rest of the time, when they were doing it for their own benefit rather than ours, was a moot point. Reinard was such a gentle man at heart, of such kind spirit, and in that forgivable way that people sometimes are, thrilled at the thought that here he was living someone else's reality for a little while. Still, I couldn't help but ask.

'But save it from what, Reinard? And for who? The Moken, or for you?'

The thought had never been far from my mind, a worry that we were all just wasting our time, running headlong from one whim to the next and never with any thought as to where it all was going.

'Please just tell me,' I begged, ever so slightly. 'What's your idea for whatever we film down there, or up here, or on the beach? Do you have any thoughts about what you even want to convey?'

He looked at me, hurt that I was yet to understand. 'You know the plan. To bring back wisdom.'

At least if Reinard had been an acid casualty he'd have made more sense, I could have placed his oddity to some excess of the eighties, but as it was, he was simply an unusually idealistic man from Luxembourg. I stopped my eyes rolling, bit my tongue, spoke from my throat so as not to let my true feelings barrel up out of my chest.

'I know that's what you want to do. But *how* Reinard, *how* do you plan to do that?'

He paused. Confronted by such straight terms, he was stumped. The compressor went on pounding, the hose feeding out as Reinard stammered and then responded.

'By showing how wisdom enriches lives here.'

That was my own moment to be stumped. Reinard and I were starting from different places, different planets even. His thoughts were not mine, he didn't see the things I saw, right down to the fact that the man saw wisdom where I did not. He had missed the drunk chief, the pregnant girls smoking palm leaf cigarettes, an elderly man dousing his wounds with petrol, and children playing catch among piles of smouldering plastic. For sure there was wisdom to be found on Surin, but there was also on offer, sometimes, a clear lack of the stuff.

'Look, you do not want to tell people you are presenting them with wisdom. You want them to feel it for themselves. If you tell them that's what you are doing, it's ruined. The art of delivering a message is to present a picture, and leave your message somewhere in the background for people to find there themselves, and to think that they found it for themselves. Otherwise it doesn't work.'

Reinard laughed at me, delighted with my proposal and slapping a hand to my shoulder.

'This, *this* is why I brought you here! This sort of thinking is indispensible to the success of *Earth One*.'

There's nothing worse than being called indispensible. Reinard, worryingly, thought he was paying a compliment, but as the man on the compressor began pulling in hose at a rapid rate, and a pool of bubbles grew more frantic and eventually broke with Jake's head returning to surface, the conversation was over. Reinard leant out of the boat, took the camera from Jake's outstretched hands.

'We have it?' He clamoured for an answer. 'We have the footage?'

Jake nodded, pulled the regulator from his mouth. 'Yeah, they found some stuff. They had to look quite hard, and it was dark down there, but I got it.'

Reinard clapped his hands and clenched a fist. Turning to me with a smile wide enough for the two of us, he stuck his thumb up happily, not about to turn back round until he'd got some positive reaction out of me. He grinned, I frowned, he grinned, and then I burst. I couldn't help but laugh along with the man as he slapped my shoulder again in his delight.

At the end of it, with the hose coiled back up on deck, the compressor lifted down from its perch, we handed over an envelope full of bank notes. Forty-five minutes the Moken spent on and off that seabed for us in the end; coming up with a string bag containing a shell, a sponge and a pretty-looking rock. I looked at the bag, a prop that was now redundant, lying discarded on the deck of the *kabang*. Damp spots of water glistened and then soaked into dark pools where they had trickled from inside the shell on to the dry wood. Jake packed a camera away, and one of the Moken tapped Reinard on the shoulder, pointing helpfully to the string bag. The man spoke Thai directly at Reinard, who smiled and leant in to be sure that he could hear properly the words being said in a language he didn't understand. The Moken broke it down, real simple: he pointed to the string bag, pointed to Reinard, raised his eyebrows in a question mark. They both paused. The Moken pointed to the string bag a second time, and then pointed overboard, back to the sea.

Reinard got it, laughed. 'No, no. We don't want it.'

He pointed at the water, and so the Moken picked up the bag and shook it out. With a splash, those few oddments of the sea – which the envelope of cash and half the afternoon had been spent to retrieve – went back beneath the waves, and sank slowly out of sight.

Try Not to Breathe – afternoon

Fleets of fish strafed over the water, their flying fins and tails perforating the surface for the briefest of moments. In a shade of pale red, a solitary jellyfish bobbed by, floating through like the plump nose of an alcoholic sailor. Beside it, the waters broke with the needle of a single fish leaping out and sinking back with the arch of a perfect stitch upon the sea.

Having returned briefly to the village, dropping off three of the men, we floated just below the side of *Atlanta*. Laurie took the rope from the *kabang* with a thumbs-up for the man leaning on the engine, and looped it around a wooden dowel in the rigging, tying it off so that the boats stayed close to one another.

'You got what you were looking for?' Laurie asked, as Jake passed up a case of equipment and Nim made her escape back to *Atlanta*.

'I think so, but it was murky down there.'

'Good stuff.' Laurie leant back, pointed towards a nearby cove in the lap of a small island. 'There's some decent coral and some life over there, if you wanted a good place to film the spear fishing in shallower water.'

Nim leaned over to us, wearing a dress, her black hair up in a high ponytail. She smiled, seeming happy not to be involved any longer.

'You go spear fishing now?' she asked, pointing in the same direction as Laurie.

Reinard nodded, brimming with eagerness to capture this purity of the Moken, swimming unaided underwater. He turned to one of the Moken men standing bare-chested and youthful beside him and, with palms inwards in front, motioned a dive.

'Now we go diving?' said Reinard. 'Free diving!'

Nim translated. The Moken man nodded.

Reinard smiled with contentment; the arrangement coming together nicely, this *pièce de résistance* of his film really taking shape. The Moken man spoke to Nim, and in his left hand lifted an underwater hunting contraption made from a rod of metal, a rubber band, and a dart. In his right hand he held the mask and pipe of a snorkel. Nim and the man exchanged a few words, some sense of disagreement on his face. His right hand lifted a second time, the man repeated a few words from a moment earlier, quite clearly understandable across the language barrier: 'I take the snorkel.'

Nim translated. 'He look for fish, but he not know if he catch. Sometimes no fish. He take the snorkel and swim.'

The snorkel. That right there was a sticking point. The poor man actually thought we wanted him to breathe. In the outside world, to what little extent they were known of, the Moken were reputed biologically adapted to life underwater. Moken children had been found in scientific studies to have superior underwater eyesight to Western children. They were, from days before mechanical diving equipment, renowned as exceptional free divers, and the very idea that the Moken even needed to get air while underwater was something of a disappointment to Reinard, the thought that he'd use something so banal as a snorkel made from heavy plastic, preposterous.

'Does he really need the snorkel?' asked Reinard.

Nim translated, the Moken man gave a nod and uttered a response.

'He say it make it easier to stay underwater.'

Reinard pondered. 'Perhaps just the goggles, but no pipe?'

Nim translated. The Moken man looked crestfallen, but gave a reluctant nod, and with an entirely innocent look of relief, Reinard smiled happily. After the shortest of journeys in the *kabang*, once again, we were in business.

With a splash, the Moken man dropped backwards over the side; feet and ankles disappearing. Reinard picked up a second camera and began filming as Jake again readied his own in its underwater casing. Moving around behind his lens, Reinard spoke excitedly.

'For the underwater stuff I think we could maybe get some behind-the-scenes footage, to show people how it was made.'

Jake nodded, pulling on fins as Reinard lowered himself and the camera close to the deck, so as to leave the viewer looking ever so slightly up at Jake from floor-level; thereby crowning him with the heroism of a great, towering figure. Jake pulled a snorkelling mask over his eyes, gave Reinard's camera two thumbs-up, and armed with his own camera held firmly in his hand but also strapped to his wrist, he followed the Moken into the water. Faced with the prospect of being left with Reinard once again, I took a spare snorkel, crossed to the other side of the boat, and followed over the edge.

Down I swam, hands parting in front of me, with the ocean once again the bound pages of a large book pulled laboriously open in my lap. Below and all around moved tiny schools of fish; pale white, blue as a dahlia, striped in zebra or boasting gilt edges down their spines. Butterfly fish investigated the faces of rocks below while snappers moved in groups at some distance, turning and receding in formation as they felt my blunt arrival. Fish with lances for noses twice their own length jousted past, a barracuda drifted by and urchins looked up with two crystal-like dots that seemed to peer out from the heart of foot-long needles. Moving closer, when sun burst through cloud to strike first the water and then the seabed, at the heart of those urchins there bloomed a bright, glowing asshole; orange and black and ringed with blue as if the eye of a peacock's tail. In the waters all around came rocks that blossomed like roses, bulged as if brains or were affixed by pairs of crenellated lips. Creatures stuck fast to the stone, and went painted at the edges with an electric neon that flexed and blew kisses as the energy of my waves moved against it, closing shyly again when I neared to take a better look.

The calm of it all drew me further out, looking for Jake and the Moken as I went turning corners into new neighbourhoods where there came still more iridescent fish. One neared my outstretched hand, wearing the orange and white masks of a sad clown. From the corner of my eye, I saw the waving tissues of a neon pillow case, suckling a rock and spilling green feathers on the sea as tiny fish came falling out of it to investigate my intrusion. There drifted up the thin, lilac ribbon of a sea snake swimming towards my suddenly gaping eyes and then, as it realised my own large presence, turning to trail off and away, apparently more scared of me than I was of it. The personalities of the things presented themselves: that mere, solitary word *fish* suddenly so inadequate when underwater in their kingdom and out of my own. There were those that fled, those that ignored, and then those that would stand their ground – their water – and face-off against me. A hundred times their size, still they swam headlong my way, a frantic but determined wriggling of the tailfin until their head hit against my skin and they backed off to line up for a second pass. Fish in pin stripes and polka dots moved about me, crabs walked below, dusting white sand against the open, howling faces of cavernous sponges. I swam, and never before had nature exposed itself quite so, flashed as such a beautiful, burlesque siren; a masquerade ball, an eccentric and the most pure-spirited of exhibitionists. Then, all of a sudden, a shadow fell upon the sea, and with fish spreading every which way, looming above came a freight train of the underwater world. It appeared beneath the dark, bowl-cut hair, flattened and weightless against a face with its breath held and cheeks full. Bearing down upon me were the spread hands and the kicking legs of the Moken man, powering fast towards me, his face shut-up tight as all submarine life went scarpering from his path.

Kicking and pulling hard at the water, I moved clear to one side and away from the camera's view. And there I saw a most peculiar sight, watching the profile of a long-nosed fish as it went swimming away from a Moken man who went swimming with a spear gun away from a white man swimming with a camera held before him. Camera chased man chased fish. The Moken diver had a frog-like crawl; his legs almost walking, with knees bent at irregular and untidy angles, but the unorthodox stroke so powerful that Jake, despite wearing large fins, still struggled to keep pace.

Swimming clear of them and into shallower waters, I climbed up the first rock that reached above the surface. From there, I watched the scene with the waves breaking gently around me. Occasionally the Moken man and Jake would come back up, so that the diver could breathe anew, and in the *kabang*, Reinard scurried with a camera to stay close to the action. As Jake came to the surface, full in Reinard's frame, I heard Reinard shouting, distant but excited at his behind-the-scenes footage: 'Everything looks great, really great!'

Watching him, excitable and alone in the boat, I felt I saw Reinard for what he truly was; nothing but a film student who'd never been to film school, going through the motions he'd learned watching endless well-meaning documentaries on the internet. It occurred to me that if the online world was able to provide isolated minds with unverified conspiracy and extremist visions, then so too had it given Reinard – shacked up with a modem in central Thailand – news and a very tender calling to try helping indigenous people in their struggle for survival. It wasn't that his efforts in documentary-making were any less sincere than average, only less organised. If anything, his approach maybe turned out more genuine than those successes that one day make it on to a screen; for if nobody was ever to see the events we recorded out on Surin that week, then perhaps we remained only a story ourselves, rather than the architects of one. Reinard's was just a naïve, warm-hearted desire to change the world through images, as if it were still 1920 and the movie camera had just been invented. In the end, once the sum total of our footage proved so disorganised and haphazard, and his hopes of broadcast faded, perhaps that above all else, I thought, ensured that our documentary would always remain honest. The presence of a camera behind all we view on a screen is only the consent of the viewer to be lied to; it is an unspoken negotiation, a contract by which we are allowed to enjoy what we see, so long as we are willing to forgive that the events were orchestrated for our benefit.

Up on that rock, the entire film and its meaning seemed to crystallise. In the behind-the-scenes footage Reinard went gathering eagerly, there was no effort to conceal the making of a film, but rather to parade it. That revelation was somehow the finale to the circus act we'd been in all along. Where once people had gone out to explore and map unknown lands and waters, in time they would set out instead to follow the maps and come to better understand what was already known to be there. Eventually, with land and sea well-charted for commercial and military gain, it had become valuable to document those whereabouts for a popular audience, and now that even those audience members had been empowered by the jet engine and the camera to visit and to record places for themselves, it had ultimately become of value to document also the making of the document, the art of making art. Discovery was fast running into diminishing returns, and as a result, showing the scaffolding had become part of the deal. The magic of entertainment was becoming harder by degrees to perform successfully; people were tougher to impress and less likely to be fooled, so that the next phase, the behind-the-scenes, was to promote the secrets of the trickery.

The fact of the matter was that the viewers – supreme and sovereign – were worth it, they deserved every length gone to and every ardour, no matter the effort. Maybe that was only the route to progress. In the nineteenth century, the camera had democratised pageantry, allowing families who were not indecently wealthy to pay for a photo or two displaying their existences, but only a few. Recording technology had since then become so available that a group of us, who were really very little more than tourists ourselves, were now empowered to document the outside world, with the limits of our success set entirely by our own competence and not at all by technological capability. In the end, with amateurs and the curious running amok, so much would have been seen, recorded, documented, that we would all grow intolerant of the world's problems, and the world would begin to improve. Or perhaps, conversely, we would simply grow numb. There would come a time when no artist nor documentary maker was able, willing, or themselves sufficiently moved to conjure a work or an emotion that could rouse people back home from the lethargy of what life had become.

Whatever the hopes and perils hidden in all that, it was the Moken as actors and protagonists in the film who seemed to have a role that was at the same time powerful and totally impotent. The Moken were tireless, unwitting endorsements of humankind; adverts for a world that had once worked honestly. In the vast global economy, it was their job to sit on a beach, desiring no more, entirely satisfied but equally disconnected and largely clueless of any other vision of what their lives could be. Millions of employees would watch them curiously in the evening and, furnished by that spirit, go back to work the next day having enjoyed enough stimulation to work another shift. Had someone audited the emotional value of the Moken and other peoples like them, those guys would have been priceless. They worked like silent, unpaid lobbyists for the system and its merit, where trillions of dollars kept on ticking over in the satellites above, or the fibre optic cables beneath those seas where they dived.

The cameras and tripods told the story, still more if you included those of the Japanese and Chinese tourists now and then arriving on the Surin beachhead. All those hundreds of thousand of dollars, yen, renminbi of technology and engineering went about trying to capture visual record of a man using two metal rods and a large rubber band to catch one fish. No expense spared. On land or sea, the world's peasants had become lucrative, as if they were the repository of human innocence. People had to see these beings so as to believe that we were all still good, still pure, without industrial sin, and to envisage that a better humanity still existed and had not been sold off in search of capitalist progress. Their poverty, Juy's gasoline-dressed wounds, were all slow-moving; chaos always sets in invisibly, one dull hardship at a time, and whether it was the Moken or their low-income viewer back in the West, life was made steadily more difficult by unremarkable degrees. The people of Surin, all but voiceless in this world, lived a history that was little more than a catalogue of stories that almost annihilated them, right up until one came along that actually would. Harassed by naval vessels as they crossed new-fangled marine borders, banned from catching fish to trade even as trawlers stripped the sea bare, the Moken would survive a hundred tsunamis, but could withstand the modern world for just a few more decades.

PART IV

ABOARD ATLANTA

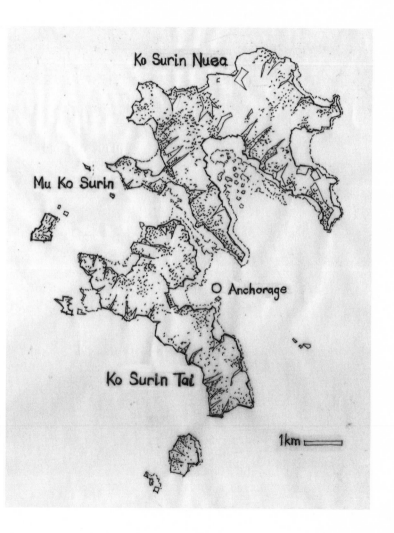

Ko Surin Nuea

Mu Ko Surin

O Anchorage

Ko Surin Tai

1km

Up the Rigging – Sunday, morning

Reinard walked towards me on deck, rubbing his hands together. The diving scenes had put a spring in his step: he seemed flattered by the technology at our disposal, less interested than ever in what overall story or message we had in mind. He opened his mouth, with a few seconds seeming to pass before any word appeared.

'I think things are really coming together with the film now. All we need is the book. I thought maybe you could start work on it, while we're still all together.'

'You want a book?'

He nodded. 'Or maybe a script, for the narrator to read.'

'I didn't know we had a narrator.'

'We don't, not yet. But I thought it would be a good idea to have a famous person who would narrate it. That would help us gain more interest in the project.'

'OK. Do we have a famous person?'

Reinard shook his head.

'Well, then do you want a script or a book?'

'I'm not sure. Which do you think?'

I gave a smile, there was nothing in his wishes to engage with. Reinard just wanted some words.

'A script and a book are quite different things. I'll just stay back on *Atlanta*, and start making notes. How's that?'

Reinard smiled the smile of a plan coming together, rested his hand on my shoulder. 'That's great, that's really great.'

From the boat, I began making the notes that eventually became this book; *Atlanta* suddenly a more peaceful place with only Laurie and me aboard. Across the deck I would notice the patterns of his day more closely, so imagining the habits he had developed during a life on water. From the hammock he spent most waking hours just watching the sea, coming to identify local islands, rocks and currents with the same familiarity you or I would notice turnings in the streets. Beaches that appeared and disappeared with tides, the density of forest on a small rock, the crags of a mountain; the location and time of day that each mark corresponded to made sense to him as clear as any road sign.

For all the small intricacies and curious details, those days would come to feel so long, as if each hour passed twice. On board you had sufficient time, and insufficient distraction, so that it was rare not to find yourself returning to an idea repeatedly. Whether it was about the Moken or something else, you could think one idea, then another, and then return to the first, forgetting and remembering and then forgetting again so many times that it took a moment to realise the sun had neither set nor risen since the first time the thought had occurred to you. For want of any distraction, everything that did happen seemed somehow more interesting and dramatic; a bird diving into the sea, a fish jumping out – small things stayed with you. I wondered whether this was the cause of the famously tall stories of those who lived at sea. The details in those tales grew ever more lifelike, the numbers ever larger, because so very little else happened to keep them in check. The stories in the end were not quite the truth, but nor were they lies, because they were reported in the most honest of fashions, and with only the sincere enthusiasm of a captive audience intoxicated by the eternal glory of a good story.

In these ways, life on the boat teased your circadian rhythm, and once you realised that the sense of boredom was only the manifestation of your own impatience, you made peace with the arrangement, and it could come to feel like time was being slowly given back to you. After a few days watching it from *Atlanta*, I came to see Surin as little different; only a slightly larger boat, more stable and made of sand, another small geography painting a tiny fleck of white and green against the pale blue blouse that dressed the skin of the earth.

Living on land it had always been easy to make water abstract, the sea a realm alien to our existence. To most of us, it was only one vast and mysterious black-blue box, and though we had perhaps gazed out to it, or paddled in its waters, our relationship with it in those moments was never with feet far from dry land. It was hard to care, still less to care deeply, for a thing that felt so remote. In listening to Laurie and the Moken, and to a lesser extent even Erik and Reinard, what happened was that their unthinking respect and love for the marine world began to rub off. To them, that relationship was a thing so implicit they felt no need to explain it, but just assumed everyone cared as much as they did, and recognised the great and pressing need to reverse the damage to the world's oceans and fish stocks. It was through being exposed to their sense of priorities that you realised they were not your own, and began to question why not.

Sometimes I would wonder what it was that Laurie and the Moken had in common; if it was only the sea and their nomadic calling, or something more than that and soon to be extinct. However different their lives and lineages, both existed for the stories and the simplest pleasures life had to offer. The world was a straightforward place to Laurie, not one of spirits and incense, but nevertheless a land of good guys and bad guys, with hidden plots to uncover which explained it all. Whatever the similarities, Laurie and the Moken were differently endangered. Apart from his passport, skin and mother tongue, the main contrast between them, as is maybe always so between the world's relative richer and poorer, was an inequality of vision. Laurie had grown up – furnished by books and history – accepting that all the world was his to roam. The Moken did not think in those terms, of places so far afield, and they were willing to settle for far less. For sure the entire sea was theirs, and its emotional reach universal to them as a touchstone, but the globe outside of local waters did not really figure in their view. Perhaps a part of it was nothing more complex than engineering; the schooner *Atlanta* was fit to travel further than the *kabang* of the Moken. Beyond that, and for all of his willingness to live a spartan life, Laurie had that Western trait where, sick of our comforts and conformity, a little adventure and a dose of hardship are things a certain type of person begins to crave. Hardship was something the Moken life would never need seek out.

One afternoon, a few rainclouds gathering on a stiff wind, and the rest of the crew on Surin, I remember watching as Laurie wrestled with a snared rope high up a mast. Barefoot, he clambered neatly up the rigging, then leant all the way across, some ten metres above the deck, where he steadied himself with one hand and went at the rope with the other. Just as he had been off the front of the boat with the jib sail in the storm, at times like that he would become ageless in his disregard for risk, ever so slightly immortal. Other times he would talk about labouring for money or worrying about the volatility of Nim's moods, and my heart ached a little to realise that he was in fact already old and tired. His age, I suspected, was my concern before it was his. Laurie was fine, Laurie would always be fine … even at the last hypothetical moment of falling headlong from the deck of *Atlanta*, to be drowned, dashed upon rocks and then lost forever … still Laurie would have been OK. He wouldn't have been worrying for himself. In him was the notion, captured perfectly, that if a person should jump to their death from a high building, then at some point before hitting the ground, they smile.

Although he'd have gone down happy in a whirlpool, put up a firm fight and gouged hard at the eyes of a great white shark, you could see that the idea of dying in a bed, sick or infirm, scared the man. To be honest, it scared me too. Laurie was one of those people who outlines the greater parameters of life, and you had to be afraid that life itself would shrink back down without him and the riches of his experience. His commitment to his spirit, to a passion for the world, its environment and its people … there was something about it that delineated the limits of what a life could be. It was heartening and reassuring to be in the presence of that, accompanied by a worry that he was the last of his kind. The twentieth century had lapped against Laurie like the waves on *Atlanta*'s bow. It had smoothed him, angered him, tired him, but his spirit was intact.

As the hours passed, now and then he would get up, walk the deck and lazily let a bucket drop on the end of its rope into the sea. It would land with a splash that upended it, before sinking down to fill so that Laurie could lift it back one rope knot at a time. Repeatedly he would tip that water on to the deck, and it ran in dark streams that spread out against *Atlanta*'s white, sun-scorched wood.

'What are you doing?' I asked once, watching curiously from a small puddle of shade.

'Soaking it. The water stops the wood contracting too much as it dries in the sun. Once that happens then you can end up with big gaps emerging in the deck. But you can only soak it with salt water.'

I laughed at the stern tone of his warning, Laurie so meticulous about the upkeep of that boat.

'I mean it! With fresh water down there in the wood you can get rot setting into the timbers. What the salt's doing is keeping it all sterile, so that you don't get any bacterial life in there.'

'So, basically, you're pickling it?'

'That's it, Jules … you got it.' And he gave a light laugh, as was his way when he realised something to have been plainly understood.

'You're looking forward to getting off the boat and back to dry land?' he asked.

'I dunno, it's nice without everyone on board.'

'You betchya it is.'

'How about you, you're looking forward to sailing home?'

'I've got a long list of repairs on *Atlanta* that never gets any shorter, I suspect I'll press on with that lot.' And he gave a smile. 'Get back to the mosque waking me up at five in the morning.'

I thought a moment, went back to that old subject from earlier in the week. 'You know lots of people are Muslims but don't worry about going to pray? I've got family in Turkey who, I guess, are Muslims … but they're no more religious than you. Then I know other Muslims who just go out to work and pay the mortgage and are actually quite boring.'

Laurie's eyes rolled a little. You could tell he didn't like confrontation with friends, but also knew his mind to be unchangeable.

'It's like I said, Jules … I know you're only looking out for your own, but I've seen what I've seen.'

On and off, we continued to talk politics, often agreeing in principle but not detail about where the world was heading, and the reasons for it. Of all things, stubborn as you like, he could only ever be sure he was right. The same certainty that loved to sail *Atlanta* close to the wind and up to the apex of towering waves, was also a certainty that would countenance no doubt about the ways of the world, or troubled to reflect on them. He'd lived through so much that it was unfathomable to him that he might not know it all and could well have been wrong; diplomacy to him was not a natural art, so that it was as if he thought it almost a form of dishonesty.

In his certainty that there was a conspiracy to take over the planet, or specifically to enslave society under Sharia law, Laurie's worldview sounded similar to reports that had begun to take root in populations all over the world, and certainly back home in Britain. His life showed what happens when a person spends so long without a society and others around him, but what felt strange, however, was that the isolation of a man who had lived decades on a boat in the tropics was now scarcely any greater than that of those who lived in crowded cities and worked production-line jobs but never talked to one another. The internet was coming to educate us all in the same truths and falsehoods, giving everyone an opportunity only to reaffirm what they already believed.

When I listened to his prejudices, sometimes, to keep the peace,

I had to give him the benefit of the doubt, thinking that the principles of a better world are born of living in a protected and more comfortable one. Laurie had been exposed to a life less padded; he had seen more blood and guts, encountered more pirates, those on the margins who were driven by necessity, poverty, addiction and rapacious ends. He'd been ripped off and hoodwinked, threatened and intimidated, and his views were only a product of that. I wondered what would come of the values in many liberal minds had they shared his experiences. In the cities of richer countries, we depended on the fact that far flung corners – those peripheries from which our resources were extracted – would remain at safe distance, and we relied on that proxy far more than our lives or thoughts would ever willingly acknowledge. The violence of the world was played out elsewhere.

Other times, I tried hard to make sure I wasn't just making excuses for him. Laurie was a man who spoke English, carried powerful passports, and as such was more privileged than the vast majority of those he'd lived around. And yet still he felt threatened, convinced that his way of life was under attack, and despite the fact that he lived free to wake each morning in an existence he thought by and large to be paradise. For all that I tried not to judge him for some of his opinions, it did make me sad that Laurie would have enjoyed his time on earth no less without the more prejudiced ones, and as a white man he'd never had to be burdened by that sort of discrimination that would keep others – including some of those he loved or had loved – restricted, fearful for their rights in ways that he could never have abided.

Only of Islam could I not speak to him, and even then, not because either of us was unwilling to do so, only that I found his hatred for the religion and its people oppressive. Muslims were written like a caveat in his heart, and in a man with so much love in him, I found the animosity there too sad and too troubling in what it meant for one billion of the world's people, auguring a war or persecution with the potential to drown even the bloodshed of the twentieth century. A part of me suspected that an imagined threat of Sharia law and Islam were just fulfilling the eternal human need for mythology and a sense of peril, but that was little comfort.

Even there though, in time I would realise that it was the idea and not the reality that troubled him. A few years later I met with Laurie on the Malay island of Langkawi, and one morning we sat together eating a breakfast of rice and curry. I was moving on, waiting to take a boat to Penang and then the Malaysian mainland, while Laurie was stopped in for tax-free fuel. Suddenly, from across the table, he was smiling brightly at something over my shoulder. He gave one of his customary and well-pronounced winks, his head turning into it. I looked over to the next table, where a young woman, head covered tightly by a headscarf, was setting down the tray with her meal, looking towards us and with a bright smile of her own.

'What is it?' I asked.

He shook his head, gave a deep chuckle as he remarked, almost as if for the richness of the world and all the people in it.

'Such a beautiful smile.'

'Who?'

'I just had a good thirty seconds' eye contact with that lady there,' and he laughed happily, 'locked right on to one another we did.'

And you could feel it was as if his very soul had been warmed by the encounter, recharged. That was life to him, and the headscarf and faith an irrelevance of the human wearing it.

Up Anchor – Monday, evening

We readied to leave Surin beneath a perfect deluge, bullets of rain shooting down from the sky and then ricocheting back as they hit sea. Raindrops raced side by side, others collided in dogfights; mid-sky they blew one another to smithereens. A large wasp, its sting dragging through the air behind it, flew to the edge of a palm leaf that ran with white marbles of water, the wasp's legs attaching as it walked round to the underside of the leaf to shelter. Swallows appeared from each cranny and corner of the village and forest, looping and gliding in ecstatic arcs, sickles and crescents, their wings beating fast and then hugging back at the side of their breasts as they cut over the air and swept down to hide among the earth. Beneath the wide, waxy leaves of a short tree, a finch sought cover, hopping on the steep branch of smooth, slippery bark and then ruffling its feathers with a half beat of the wing in an attempt at staying dry. Raindrops hit violently against the oldest of yellow flowers growing above the leaves of another tree, their petals fell loose and sometimes pulled the whole flower down to earth in the prettiest of parachutes. Against that backdrop, somehow the sun broke out of the cloud, shone hot through the soaking and eternally falling sky, so that both rain and sunlight for a moment co-existed and managed to share all the horizon happily as one.

Further off in the distance, a darkening bank of cloud hung back, as if we were seeing only the dress rehearsal of a greater storm coming. The wind beat the waves against *Atlanta*, asking us to leave and whistling a tune through the rigging, humming to us: *Looka yonder! A big black cloud come! A big black cloud a-come!* Nim had left a further envelope of pumpkin seeds for Moo Hning's family, promising that they would grow well in the Surin earth. Moo Hning was given a banana plant by her relatives, its root heavy with soil and Moo Hning holding it to her front as she waded with the others back to the dinghy with the plant in a plastic bag. Together with Erik, Jake and Reinard, she and Pho Nau made their way through the shallows, pushing the small boat to deeper water until they hopped over the sides and lowered the outboard, propelling them back out to *Atlanta*.

For a couple of days before we left, Moo Hning and Pho Nau became positively metropolitan in their concern for punctuality. They'd triple-checked the plan for departure, made absolutely sure we knew which hut they were in should there have been any complication. 'Don't leave without us' had been translated so many times that it was coming to sound familiar even in Thai. Whatever their ancestry, they had no wish to be stranded with it. The speed at which they made it out to the dinghy corroborated Laurie's certainty that any family with enough money, or network in a town, always hot-footed it off places like Surin, and on to Phuket.

As the crew returned from Surin a final time, Jake climbed back aboard and shook his head impatiently, with only Reinard still seeming buoyed at the prospect that he really was making movies. Looking frustrated, Erik gave a sigh, rolled his eyes knowingly in my direction.

'Rough day?' I asked, to which he shrugged.

Jake lifted his cameras from his back and walked below deck, not troubling to look round as he muttered to himself. 'It's a goose chase, that's all.'

Under sail and also with that pound of the engine, we left Surin, its shape getting gradually small and faint. The storm must have been blowing a different course to ours as *Atlanta* headed south for Rawai, and soon we had moved into clearer skies where the late afternoon sun pressed towards the sea, tiring as it fell downwards in the sky. Under winds growing more favourable, the engine was cut, and Laurie looked out over the horizon as *Atlanta* pressed forwards at her usual tilt. The sails filled, leaning us over one way while the rudder tilted us the other, so that between the two opposing forces we held a straight course with the boat slanting right down into the water, inviting the sea to wash down one side of the deck where Nim trailed her feet. Laurie pressed his hand to the side of the coach house, spoke slowly with the tenderness of a memory.

'Maldives is about a week and a bit of sailing from here going west, at this time of the year, with good winds.'

'What's it like, being out in the middle of the Indian Ocean or the Pacific for that long?'

He kept looking at the horizon.

'It's a freedom, mate. You're in your own domain. You're catching fish, all you need to keep you healthy is limes, coconut, rice. It's something that's just magic, it really is. When you're crossing an ocean, you get out there, and it takes two or three days to settle into it, but once you do … it's just beautiful. You're at one with nature, with the movement of the boat. You're down in the galley cooking your food, or you're splicing a rope, setting a sail, fighting a storm. It's all just the way it should be. And then, when I get in close to port, I get a bit worried, I think "fucking hell … I'm going back to that, to that bloody civilisation again".'

Laurie shook his head. 'One of the hard parts is that, when you come back in, after you've been out there … you've been so at one with yourself. Whether you've had a partner or a mate on board, you've been one with the world out there. And your brain is so clean, and it's so clear.'

For a moment he said nothing, as if the fragility of that world were damaged just by uttering the thought.

'And coming back into port, you've got this fucking immigration and customs bureaucrat, and every time they think that they're reading you. *They* think they're reading *you*. And yet you know exactly what they're going to ask before they can even get it out of their head, because you're so far into theirs. And that's how it goes, that first contact with someone's mind when you've had nothing in your own but the world. No judgements, no nothing, just peace. Face to face – you know right then what it is you're coming back to, 'cos you're looking right into it, with these fools asking you these stupid questions, thinking that you're carrying drugs and all that shit.'

'Like there's automatically a negative assumption in there?'

'Exactly!' Laurie snapped at it, that way he sometimes did when it seemed I'd said something more precisely, in fewer words than he'd thought it himself.

'What do you think you'd have done if you hadn't wound up on boats?'

Laurie's nose lifted with a little disdain, the thought incomprehensible.

'There wasn't ever gonna be any other way for it.' He turned and looked at me seriously. 'So many times, Jules, and I ain't superstitious, but if I wasn't meant to have been on boats, and lived this life, then I don't understand that time off Jamaica when I was looking for a place to drop anchor for the evening, and I point at this cove and say to my mate, "Looks like there's about five fathoms in there."

'And I shit you not, Jules … right then a Jamaican fisherman comes paddling up in his boat, sees that we're trying to figure it out, and he points to the cove and says, "Go in there … deep water, five fathoms."'

Laurie let out a short burst of laughter, then simply smiled.

'I don't know why, but I guess they always just drew me in a bit like that, boats and the water. I was born in the middle of a war … 1943 … and all my earliest memories are of this bombed-out city, playing in the rubble of London. And there were damn doodlebugs still circling overhead and an air raid shelter at the bottom of the garden, the Battle of Britain just getting started. My dad was a steeplejack back then, and after the war he used to put up signs for businesses all over the city. He got around in a motorbike and sidecar, and I used to jump in the sidecar and, looking up, I'd see the city from down there. And it was mad, man, it was a mess. The whole place was destroyed, fucking ruined. My parents moving to Australia was the best thing that could have ever happened to me. I don't know what I'd have become in London. We moved to outside Melbourne, and there were fields, horses, paddocks and dinghies to paddle the rivers in. And there was so much space.'

He said it with what was almost a sigh of relief, like he could still feel those expanses. In his voice then, when Laurie described the relief of leaving a depressed and war-ravaged London for the peace and new life available in Australia, it was hard not to consider the way the modern world had denied the victims of war in the Middle East and North Africa that same opportunity of sanctuary and new beginnings. Where the Europeans of the twentieth century had been welcomed to build anew; to go to the United States, Canada, Australia, where they had seen the lands of Palestinians seized and given over to make Israel, we had become a world, numb to morals and history, that left victims of war to grapple with the psychological wounds of conflicts still raging and in rubble all around.

Laurie sipped from a mug of water. 'I remember getting on to that steamer bound for Australia, and I was eight years old and looking up at the steel rivets shining on the chimney. And even though it wasn't a sail ship they still had rigging in those days, to mount the derricks on, for loading and unloading the hull. The masts were so high, Jules, and I was just a young lad stood at the bottom of them and looking up, so high. And I couldn't help but climb the things, just like at school I'd always had to keep drawing pictures of boats when I was supposed to be studying. I just had to climb that rigging, even though it sent my mother crazy.'

He looked round at me, sad but mesmerised. 'And twenty years before me it was the wind. Twenty years before and they didn't even have the steam engines. And then when I was in Port Lincoln, watching the grain come down the river, in from the fields. The wheat and the barley all stacked in hessian sacks on the back of sailing ships. You could see the crew unloading each time, at the end of that journey downriver, from the wheat fields of the interior, where the ear of the crop leans the stalk right over before harvest. And I'd watch those boats unloading, with the wind pushing full into the sail of the next one coming in, so that the canvas was almost beating from out of the mast. And I knew it … I knew it even then.'

Gitano 2.0 – Tuesday, dusk

Climbing from the dinghy to the quay we stepped back on to Rawai, the sound of car engines and horns moving along the sea road. A little way beyond, the tourists lined up, their clothing marked with the coloured stickers the ferry staff placed on them to identify which island and thus boat the paying passenger was meant for. Each one badged, corralled into separate herds. I watched metal gates channel farang one way and the other and then clang shut behind them. The cattle made its way to market, the rusty gates singing with sounds of livestock for the world's most valuable commodity.

Outside a nearby travel agency was a board containing a handful of adverts for popular trips. One was an underwater scene with farang diving among coral and tropical fish, another showed a turtle pulling up on to the sand to lay an egg, the final one had the Moken sitting on the beachfront of Surin, so you could visit those humans with their own culture, language, worries and tradition in a trip no different to one to a beach well known for turtles. The Moken were just another tourist attraction, kept going by food aid as an exhibit in an open-air zoo, where the cages were built from laws that disregarded their existence and from borders over which distant despots squabbled.

Gitano met us back where he'd left us a week earlier, Jake and I both a little thinner for those seven days, a few kilograms of weight left behind for the journey home. We lowered ourselves back into that old car, its bodywork dusted with sand and rust and sitting right down over its wheels. Silently we went, Gitano holding his tongue, like he didn't trust himself not to say anything that wasn't offensive, and anything he had in mind not really worth that risk. Motor scooters passed by outside the car window, moving backwards behind our pace: one with chickens in wire coops strapped to the flanks, another with a block of ice, a frozen menhir with a plastic sheet over the top and the thing trailing drips of water on the journey to whichever bar or restaurant had ordered it. I looked over at Gitano: his arms with their bracelets and charitable bands, the petrol gauge showing just a little above red, and the numbers now reading 200,328 kilometres. I remembered that moment after the airport, watching the gauge rise up through 200,000. Three hundred and twenty-eight of Gitano's kilometres was all that that week on Surin had boiled down to, and I wondered where they might have taken him. In front of us a truck drove slowly, the back of it open to reveal a small group of workers seated in the rear, their arms resting on the tailgate, shaded by the heavy fabric of the hood. Gitano overtook it wide on the opposite side of the road, going into the sands at the edge of the asphalt, so that a veil of dust shot up behind and beside us, falling as we retook the road surface and drifting down like a curtain call.

It almost goes without saying that no documentary was ever made, all of it still stowed safe but never to be viewed, kept aboard a hard drive and some memory cards that would bear eternal witness to the well-meaning but futile exercise it had constituted. Reinard never found a translator, meaning that Nim's rough rendering of the interviews was the closest we ever got, with no possibility of subtitles because we were clueless as to at what moment the Moken person we'd recorded was saying what. Occasionally I heard from Reinard, good-natured as always, with a new hare-brained idea, generally a variant on how he intended to secure funds for our old voyage together across the Pacific. From time to time he would write to me in the hope of getting in touch with Jake, trying to enlist his camera expertise for a 'musical journey' that, once again, would apparently explain the indigenous world to the modern.

Years later I went back to Ko Lanta to meet Laurie and listen more to the stories of his life, honouring a feeling that they should be collected for a world that no longer produced such lives as his. At the age of seventy-three he'd had a son with Nim, finally a boy to give the name Julian, and after a prolonged and volatile period of postnatal depression let go of its hold on Nim, the two of them calmed and got on with raising their small family. Laurie had lost none of his faith in his ability to look after himself just fine, but it was with a rare trace of fear that he told me he had to stick around, that he needed to stay alive another ten years to make sure Julian was supported.

When, over dinner one evening, I mentioned the tough chicken in the soup at Surin, he laughed that he'd bought a pressure cooker and had adopted a strategy of boiling the life out of old birds, so that he no longer had any trouble with them. At the time, he was struggling with a tooth cavity causing him a good deal of discomfort, and I watched as – mouth open, head tipped back – he dipped cotton wool in vinegar, forced it into the cavity, and then coated it with drops of superglue, assuring me that the glue was inert and would suffice until he made his next trip to the mainland, where a cheaper dentist could be found.

On that visit I realised, watching Laurie work at a sewing machine to repair the canvas cover that lined the sides of the dinghy, that his only capital was *Atlanta* and an understanding of how to sail her. By then, he had started passing on some of that knowledge to a teenage apprentice – half-Thai, half-British – and was patiently teaching the youngster the ways of the schooner. I watched as Laurie showed him the knots and the positions of the sails, so dutiful in sharing the tradition and his knowledge. His increasing age had only made him more grandfatherly, and with patience and time of day, he listened to questions, still answering in caring tones, never condescending to anyone.

At the time he was preparing for the start of the tourist season, his pension little more secure than a presumption that the farang would keep taking an interest in boat trips, and that the wind would keep blowing to fill his sails. Saudi funding of mosques in Thailand had continued apace, and his greatest grievance was that the call to prayer had become amplified by loudspeaker from the minaret opposite his bedroom window. Not one to take such an affront lying down, Laurie had risen early one dawn, awoke before the imam and climbed twenty feet up the concrete telephone pole, putting his old training as an electrician to good use and watching for which of the dozen or more wires that served his street was first to vibrate with the coming of electricity for the loudspeaker. As the cable began to thrum, high in the air and cutters set, Laurie told me how he'd agonised over whether or not to cut the thing, eventually deciding it wasn't the right way to go about the wider struggle against global Wahhabi Islamism. A few years later, a referendum on the island had proven him right, with locals voting in opposition to that amplification of the call.

Events would eventually return Erik to Alabama. He called time on Asia after the sea finally got him, falling into the Straits of Malacca while delivering a yacht to Malaysia. 'Top heavy' was what Laurie had once said of Erik, 'his weight was in his head and he was slow on his feet.' The poor bastard had tumbled overboard in the middle of the night, a high wave rising up, knocking him overboard as the yacht rose with it. The boat on autopilot, it had motored on and wrecked itself on rocks, with Erik fortunate to have fallen into the sea with his dry bag over his shoulder, so that he had been able to fashion a float for himself.

Eight hours he had drifted in the dark, before washing ashore on an inhabited island where he was hospitalised for a week in acute shock but lucky to be alive. Nor had his good fortune ended there, for the mishap had been set in motion by that old determination of Erik's to take on tasks in which he had no great competence. It tran-spired that Erik had purchased fraudulent sailing licences to captain the yacht to its new owner and, doubling his unlikely luck, the insur-ance company never checked the documents, meaning they paid out for the boat and got Erik off the hook without millions of dollars in unpayable debts. I wondered what would have gone through Erik's mind as he drifted all those long hours of night. I wondered if he replayed the moment with the anchor in the hull, with the gasoline and the siphon; if he'd rued all those efforts to pass himself off as experienced, or if he simply wished he'd never left Alabama.

Jake and I shook hands at the airport, returning to formality. Among the disorganisation, the two of us had been booked on separate flights out of that hot, cramped terminal, and in truth I was glad to be relieved of the awkward obligation to make more conversation. With Jake, no matter what happened, you never got whiff of a judgement; it was as if he saw emotions as something to refrain from giving his energy to. Somewhere behind the surface of his grey eyes though, in that airport, I saw a recognition process-ing. Brutally honest, he knew he'd been wasting his time and he was, that very moment, making a point of resolving not to do so in future. Right then he was already filing everyone aboard *Atlanta* as reminder of a wasted opportunity he had no wish to recall, like we were all poor souvenirs from a bad working holiday. After a few civil words, he gave a single nod of the head. He turned on his heel, walked off through the terminal, his figure obscured by the huge bag of equipment, bursting at the seams with the potential to record, store and edit realities. Most of the kit was strapped to his back, his head peering above it and still a little pink from sun. The rest he held under one enormous arm, and into the crowd he walked away.

Acknowledgements

This book owes a debt of gratitude to Patti Seery and her boat, *Silolona*, for their support of the original trip to Surin. Thanks too are owed to Laurie and to Nim for both the stories and their hospitality on the boat *Atlanta* and the island of Ko Lanta. It is also for Marco, and his unbounded enthusiasm for all things of the marine world. I would hope that the book can bring greater attention and concern for the difficulties and needs of the Moken of the Andaman Sea, and their compatriots, the Bajau, who live by similar traditions in the waters of Indonesia and Malaysia. It goes without saying that their greater story, and struggle, is integral to this very small one. Finally, I would like to give thanks to John Berger, the memory he leaves us with, and his many beautiful and insightful ways of seeing in this world.